Edna's Story -
memories of life in a Children's Home
and in Service, in Dorset and London

by Edna Wheway

Edited by Gillian Hill
Word and Action (Dorset)

Word and Action (Dorset) Ltd.
43 Avenue Road, Wimborne, Dorset BH21 1BS
Telephone: Wimborne (0202) 883197

First published in 1984 by Word and Action (Dorset) Ltd.

Acknowledgements:

The Author gives special thanks to Miss Tempe Woods
for her help and encouragement.
Thanks to Dawn Brecken,
a Senior Clerk of Social Work Administration
and Miranda Melbourn,
the Archivist of the Children's Society
for researched information
and photographs of St. Faiths.

Photographic assistance - John Palmer
Cover layout - Martin Pearce
Typesetting - Ruth Hecht

Wheway, Edna
Edna's story.
1. England - Social life and customs - 20th century
I. Title
942.082'092'4 DA566.4

ISBN 0-904939-31-6

Printed by Beckett, Bournemouth

Word and Action (Dorset) Ltd. was started in 1972 in Dorset as a community theatre and publications co-operative.

The group grew out of the nationwide movement in Community Arts which challenged the outdated belief that culture is the property of a highly educated minority, to be found only in the theatres, arts centres and museums of our larger cities; or between the glossy covers of an expensively promoted book.

Word and Action's approach to writing is one of acceptance rather than criticism. We do not aim to provide expert advice for aspiring professional writers, but to encourage ordinary people to write as freely and honestly as possible.

Word and Action (Dorset) Ltd. is a non-profit distributing co-operative subsidised by the Arts Council of Great Britain, and is a member group of the Federation of Worker Writers and Community Publishers.

CONTENTS

v Introduction

1 Beginnings

9 Daily Pattern

28 Events

37 'Memory is a rag-bag...'

47 Leisure

57 War

62 Changes

71 Dorset and Paddington

83 Chelsea

94 New Beginnings

Cover: Edna, aged 4 years

Introduction

In 1983 at the age of 80, Edna first approached Word and Action (Dorset) with her autobiography, in four parts. At once we became fascinated by the detailed memories which Edna recalled, and by her image of memory as a rag-bag - an article she used frequently, made from pieces of material and in which other oddments for mending were kept.

Due to financial limitations, Word and Action (Dorset) was able to publish only the first part, dealing with her life up to her marriage. During the process of editing we worked closely with Edna and a friendship developed. We visited regularly and delighted in the thin bread and butter and the tea in fine china cups which she learnt to present with perfection during her life in service.

Edna describes the intricate pattern of her daily life, yet her story is more than history: she has continued to develop and consider it almost to the day of going to print.

Gillian Hill and Liz Reeve
Word and Action (Dorset), May 1984

Biography

Edna Wheway was born in London in 1903. She moved to St. Faiths Home, Dorset in 1906 after her father's death. She left to go into service as a between-maid in 1919. She married in 1927 and had two children and now has three grand-daughters and two great-grandchildren. After her husband's death she moved to Southampton, where she worked for W. H. Smith on Southampton station for several years. She also became involved in the local Writers' Circle and the Natural History Society. In 1962 she married Harold Wheway, a railway worker. She twice visited Australia to visit her daughter who had emigrated. In 1972 Harold died. Edna was a founder member of the New Milton Community Centre Writing Group and wrote for the Natural History Society. She has given talks and continues at 81 to write.

Edna's family: (l. to r.)
Edna, her eldest sister Churl
(Nellie Frances), her mother,
and elder sister Ruby

Edna's father

Beginnings

It was 1906 when our father died; mother was then left with three little girls - the eldest, Churl (Nellie Frances) was six years old, Ruby was four and I was three. In those days there were no grants or benefits yet something had to be done to enable mother to cope. An agonising decision had to be made: should she part with one of her girls, and if so, which one?

During that time we lived in Stoke Newington in the Borough of Hackney. No pictures come to mind of my early life there: no feel of a mother's comforting presence, a father's care or sister's company - only a faint glimmer of something trivial: there is just one impression, not of any person or recognisable place, but of a hot day and brass lettering above a shop reflected in the dry asphalt pavement - somehow I know it was not a wet surface. How strange that this still lingers in the back of my mind after all these years.

Then fate took a hand and a decision was made: being the youngest I was the chosen one. I was accepted by a society which bore the name The Church of England Waifs and Strays Society. This society, which is today known as The Children's Society, gave people who supported them the following prayer printed on card: 'Lord, we pray thee to watch over and keep from evil the children in our Homes, and bless us in our desires to support and help them.'

I was found a place in a Home in Parkstone, Dorset. During the thirteen years that I remained there, my sisters were looked after by relatives for a while and went, in later years, to live with mother. In many ways I think I was the luckiest of the three.

Not a glimmer remains of the train journey from London. The first door which memory opened for me leads to a rather dark-looking room in which I clung to the only familiar thing I knew: the hand of the lady who had brought and 'delivered' me to the Home. The first words I can recall hearing were: 'Come and meet Louie, you are to be friends.'

A small fair-haired girl was being propelled towards me. She held her head slightly to one side, a gesture she kept for many years in moments of indecision. We stared at each other and went into a dark room to play among a lot of other girls. The room seemed to be full of them.

Louie and I remained the two youngest for several years. We were quite different from each other in appearance: Louie was slight with rosy cheeks due to a chest condition; she had green-grey eyes and fair straight hair. I was of sturdier build, pale complexion, dark curly hair and large blue eyes with a tendency to hang my head when spoken to by strangers. Although we were considered friends we did not really like each other much, yet we were always paired off together.

We did not fully understand why we were living in a Home, or who paid for our food, clothes and other necessities of life. In those days no State aid or National Health scheme was available. The magazine 'Our Waifs and Strays' invited donations to help with the placement of children; some readers held themselves responsible for the upkeep of their individual charges. A few parents did contribute what they could: although we were considered orphans a number of girls like myself had one parent living. Fund-raising by adults took many forms: drawing room meetings, fetes; we had several devices ourselves for raising funds: sales-of-work, annual Pound Day, concerts and Anniversary Day.

The name of the Home was St. Faiths although it was always called 'The Home'. The house stood on a corner of a quiet cul-de-sac and the main Bournemouth to Poole road. There was a green wooden gate at the front entrance in Mount Road and the back entrance, set in high black corrugated fencing, had a wooden board across it announcing: 'St. Faiths O Home' - the letter 'O' still showed faintly white where once the word 'Orphanage' had been painted until it was decided that 'Home' was a less pitiful word. The pale cold-looking stone of the front walls was redeemed by a creeper which turned a glorious colour in the autumn. Creamy tea-roses clustered around the windows and at times tapped on the panes. One waft of their distinctive scent makes me recall those childhood days. There was a garden with a circular flower bed outside the windows of the left-hand part of the house where Miss Langley, the Superintendant lived with her sister Miss Nina and their maid, Nellie. Nellie had once been a Home-girl I believe, without relatives or friends.

On either side of the front gate were two shrubs: one was a deep red rhododendron which smelt of hot raspberry jam. In an effort to entice the bees from such heavily laden blooms, a rich almost orange-coloured gorse bush with a scent of coconuts had been planted. Waves of the perfume hung on the summer air. What a grand time those bees must have had. Hops clambered over the balcony above the front door. They had a quite different kind of smell: tantalizing, tangy, zest of living - the same effect as of pine trees on a hot day.

Because of the laurel hedge and odd pine and fir trees dotted about and stumps left in the grass, the small lawn did not really deserve its name. Mostly the grass looked starved and brown; hard knobs of fallen fir cones lay almost hidden among the pine needles which smothered any grass bold enough to try and reach the light above. We were not allowed to walk on the lawn. The paths around the edges were worn smooth; the roots made bumps which tripped walkers like me who looked more to the tops of the trees, the sky and clouds than where their feet were going. There was a wooden summer-house which opened out facing the house: it was a rectangular room with one grimy window and many cobwebs. It had stout supporting poles to which some girls tried to add brightness by secretly sowing nasturtium seeds which did their best but seldom bloomed. Until the summer was well-advanced the house smelt damp and woody: a lovely place for crawley buttons: shiny, black rain-beetles, spiders and ants.

Down along the side, bordering the pinewood were 'our' gardens. This stretch was divided into tiny oblong plots. No-one was compelled to have one; the youngest girls were given plots nearest the summer house and overshadowed by trees; this made it harder for them to grow anything much and seemed a bit unfair, but it kept those girls happy who liked grubbing about. Some of the girls were encouraged to work in the bit of kitchen-garden, to grow vegetables mainly for Miss Langley's household. There was certainly not enough ground to supply the Home with fresh garden produce.

Nearer the house the plots became brighter and most were bordered according to individual taste. Nearly all were restrained from spreading to the next girl's garden by a border of London Pride - dainty flowers and a rosette of pretty leaves. Above the rusty wire and heavy rope clothes-lines, a few trees did their best to grow. There was a large sycamore with a one-sided look about it which overhung the back fence.

The house had just two storeys: the dormitory was above the school room with a small balcony in the centre over the front door. French doors led out to pot plants doing their best to grow in large earthenware pots standing on a zinc-based floor.

On the left was Miss Langley's bedroom - a sort of 'Holy of Holies' to us. Down this side of the house was a blank wall with a narrow slippery path, moss-covered because it was seldom used - except when one of us wanted to get to the backyard unseen by Authority, when slipping in from the roadway.

Our side of the house had a glass greenhouse built against the wall where the flue-pipe from the school room fire helped to keep it warm. A water-butt stood at one corner to collect rainwater for the plants. At the other end of the greenhouse were piles of coal and coke. A narrow scary passage ran the width of the building, from the pinewood to the backyard.

Between the outer passage and the Home's kitchen was a larger wash-house or scullery where all rough jobs were done. Boots and shoes lined the shelves round the inner wall: polishes and brushes, cleaning items and other paraphernalia were stored here. A door led to a walk-in larder, cool and dim within.

In the kitchen there was a black-leaded, steel range. It had a boiler built in to one side which had to be kept filled with water: if it was allowed to become empty we were told it would crack. The fire shed a cosy warming glow across the room, cheerful and comforting on a cold day. The floor had black and white lino on it. A massive dresser, reaching to the ceiling, filled one side. By the window stood a large heavy plain wooden table on which all meals were prepared. The table had to be scrubbed every day.

The main room was always called the school room. It was a rather dismal place and big enough for twenty or more girls with ages ranging from four to sixteen. It was used for playing and praying, singing and sewing, dancing, reading, writing, quarrelling and every other indoor activity known to growing girls herded together. It was here we spent most of our childhood days. To us children it was a gloomy yet familiar room. Two long windows were hung with heavy dark curtains which fell askew as girls would pull and swing on them. Opposite the school room door, there was an enclosed fireplace which had a large wire fireguard with a brass top securely fastened around a metal hearth. It had two small doors with curved tops. When the fire would not draw, then and only then, the top would be opened to reveal the glowing fire. We found this fascinating especially when the flames were blue - which was a sign of snow. Only the older girls were ever allowed to touch this edifice - look out any girl who was rash enough to throw even a small piece of paper on the fire. Sometimes a few cones were put on to make it brighten up on very cold days.

Opposite the fireplace stood a fierce-looking wooden rocking-horse: dapple-gray, spotted, its ears and nostrils were lined with flaming orange-red. It swung on rods at the bottom, to and fro, sometimes rather violently if a girl wanted to use a bit of extra energy when pushing one of the little ones.The padding of the saddle had worn very thin by the continued use of little bottoms over many years. It was comforting after a childish squabble to sit on Dobbin and hug his head, rocking gently until a measure of good humour was restored: we all loved him.

Next to the rocking-horse was a dark upright piano and stool in which were kept all sorts of papers dealing with matters musical. At the bottom end of the room at floor level was a stout brown-stained board, about a foot in height and eighteen inches from the wall. This went almost the full width of the room; it was divided by strong cardboard partitions into several sections. This was for the little ones to keep their toys and odds-and-ends. It was always called the 'ends': woe betide any youngster who let her 'odds' stray into another girls 'ends'!

At the sides of the room, ranged along the walls, were wooden forms without backs to them. These and the long plain wooden table had to be well scrubbed about twice a week; these forms were drawn up to the table for mealtimes. We had enamel plates and mugs. Matron sat at a separate table where she could keep a watchful eye on our table manners. Dorothy, the Under-Matron, sat at the head of our long table. No talking was allowed at mealtimes except at Christmas, Easter and on Anniversary Day.

Pictures and texts adorned the green distempered upper part of the walls. A darker green band separated the top half from the dark brown match-boarding at the bottom. The texts were in deep-red shiny cardboard, with silvery lettering. One read: 'Be good, sweet maid, and let who will be clever do noble things, not dream them all day long, and so make Life, Death and that vast forever one grand sweet song. Charles Kingsley'.

The other one was annonymous and read: 'Christ is the head of this house, the unseen guest at every meal, the silent listener to every conversation.' Childlike, I often wondered if He smiled at some of our conversations and sympathised when the meal was not very tasty or satisfying.

Our dormitory above the school room had twelve or thirteen beds in it, each with a cheery red cover, some patchwork. Under each bed was a basket to hold our clothes, and enamel potties discreetly hidden. Floorcovering of a pretty soft pink shade was well-scrubbed - never polished. In a space in front of the fireplace was a washstand with four bowls where we would strip to the waist and wash in relays. It was some years before a bathroom was built over the larder and kitchen but in those days we were frequently asked not to waste water; 'Every drop has to be paid for, you know', we were told. It was quite usual to use washing water for the garden.

A small room near the top of the stairs was the Under-Matron's bedroom; in it was a cot for any child not well and needing extra comfort.

At one period during my girlhood, it was deemed necessary to build an extra bedroom, a sort of large glorified attic which ever after was called the New Room. The windows at the front were placed too high for us to see much unless any venturesome girls managed somehow to climb up; then they could see the lovely view down the hill through the trees. It was a pleasant sunny room and for a long time there was a lovely smell of fresh cut wood. At one time girls who had mumps or measles were kept in isolation up there, but now and then an unaffected girl would sneak up to see what they looked like with lumps on their neck, or spots all over their faces and bodies. No wonder several girls caught the infection.

Now I will introduce you to the chief personalities connected with St. Faiths. Miss Langley, the superintendant, was a remarkable woman; although she could be severe she was also understanding. No girl need fear to approach her.

In our way we were fond of her although it was not until later in life that we came to understand or appreciate her qualities.

In appearance she was slightly masculine, medium height, straight grey hair parted in the centre and worn in a bun at the back; she had light-blue eyes which softened with sympathy or twinkled with amusement; and she could see through any humbug; her nose was straight and her mouth stern. She was neat and well dressed; fashion in those days dictated subdued colours, a tiny white frill of lace at the neck of a dress and usually a large cameo style brooch. A velvet band around her neck was sometimes added on highdays - Sundays and holidays.

Miss Langley had a sister, Miss Nina: frail, gentle and simple, seldom intruding into our lives. She had short cropped hair and was small in stature. We all liked her: she was dainty and ladylike. We seemed to understand that she was a 'bit touched' as it was called in those days: 'Not all there' we said and honestly meant no harm. Very occasionally she would come to look at our needlework and a kindly word of praise from her was an honour indeed. I believe she had been a very clever needlewoman herself, especially good at fine work and embroidery. Her hands were white and smooth with long slender fingers that fluttered like delicate butterflies as she held the work which attracted her attention.

Nellie was their maid-of-all-work and a homely, sturdy and very loyal soul. She may have been dependent on them for a home but she adored her two ladies and did not like being away from them for long. She worked hard and long hours; in those days conditions of service were strict and little time was allowed for freedom to live any sort of life of one's own. I believe Nellie would have given up every moment if she thought she was needed for any reason whatever.

She had charge of Roy, a brown and black Yorkshire terrier and seldom went out without him; he was too big for a dog of his breed, so like many of us, he was in a way a cast-off.

Miss Grainge, who was Matron, had almost complete control of the girls. She was not a person to be trifled with on any account. Because of her strong personality we did not realise how short of stature and rather plump she was: her severe uniform did not wholly conceal this. She was always immaculate in blue-and-white striped dress with starched cap and apron - white and spotless - worn only in the morning; in the afternoon - navy-blue dress, stiff belt with large buckle but minus cap and apron. She had thick, glossy black hair, luxuriant and long, although I doubt if many girls ever saw her with it hanging loose. It was worn pouched in front, a tight bun at the back with strands of hair neatly coiled round it and never a hair out of place.

Never was a single naughty word unheard by Miss Grainge's sharp ears. Any attempt to skimp household tasks was noticed: if her keen eyes detected any sign of sloppiness the task would soon have to be done again. She had a strong religous streak and before coming to St. Faiths had intended to become a nun but had not received the call. Stern she undoubtedly was but very fair in her judgements though we did not always see or appreciate this - especially those who were not among her favourites. Many years later I learnt that I was considered one of them: I wonder if being a stodgy, sober child had anything to do with it; I took life very seriously.

Then there was Miss Dorothy, Assistant or Under-Matron. We all thought her very pretty because she had fair hair which curled in tendrills round her face, especially in wet weather. She was fairly tall and slim, with delicate colouring and small features. She could enjoy a laugh and joke with us when Matron was not about. She was more lenient in her control of us but then she was not much older than some of the girls who had left school but who had not yet gone into Service. She could be sharp-tempered without apparent reason.

There were three distinct groups of girls: the 'tinies' or 'little ones', - up to the age of eight, the middle girls (aged between eight and twelve) and the older girls. This last group had mainly left school and would be trained in all domestic duties although there was not much opportunity to learn to cook. I was quite grown up before I even saw a raw egg. The older girls had their own allotted tasks and each one who had left school was responsible for one of the little ones, aged from five to seven. Middle girls were given less strenuous jobs than the older ones. At the age of sixteen most of us were put into private domestic service, we seldom became shop girls. It seems funny now, but girls in service (usually called skivvies) were looked down upon by girls who served in shops, while skivvies despised shop girls.

Names and faces drift through my memory, vague and shadowy. During these early years all the girls were older than me: Winnie and Gwennie, Dora and Daisy, Laura, Gladys, Elsie and many more; all have gone their separate ways - and who knows where the pathways of life have led them.

St. Faiths Home, Parkstone -
the balcony with hops and the New Room

Daily Pattern

A strange thing happened to me on my first night at St. Faiths. I was put in a bed, the last of a row of four. Water from the basins had been emptied into a tin hip-bath which was placed rather close to my bed. During the night I became restless and somehow rolled off the bed into the bath of cold water. My pink nightie clung to my body. I was lifted out. To my horror I was given a hearty slap on my bare bottom. Young as I was, this shocked me more than the chill of the water: that part of my anatomy was not supposed to be exposed to anyone's gaze. In a strange way I was outraged and never forgot the experience. Maybe the slap had been given to warm me up and then, I suppose, I was put back into bed in a dry nightie. I shivered myself down into the bedclothes but would not cry and let all those strange girls laugh at me. I thought the person who slapped me was the one who took me to the Home and, childlike, I hated her. I was glad that she left the next day; if I had been old enough to know the words I would have said, 'Good riddance'.

I well remember the day my hair was cut off. We were told that in the interest of hygiene all the girls had it cropped short like a boy: another mark of distinction which we resented. I was too young to understand reasons: I only knew that I did not want my curls to be cut. It was soon after my arrival: somehow I was lured up to the bathroom one morning and put on the lavatory seat with the lid closed, but facing the wrong way so that Dorothy could get at my hair. I was draped in a huge towel and as soon as I saw the big shiny scissors I knew what was going to happen. I kicked and screamed and put my hands with fingers outspread across my head defying Dorothy to cut off my chestnut curls. But of what use is a five-year-old's protest against a determined adult with her orders to do a job even if she dislikes doing it? My hands were tied together with a smaller towel and a few unauthorised, rather gentle smacks gained the day and the deed was done.

Strangely, as I grew older my hair became quite dark, almost black and rather coarse and wiry. In later years this led to a happening which puzzled me for some time. During one of our prize-giving days, one of the Home's benefactors came across to me and stared hard through her lorgnette muttering, 'Blue eyes and black hair - extraordinary'; then went away. She returned later with another lady to have a look at this queer child. For some nights after this I used to ask God in my secret prayers in bed to make my eyes brown because I thought there was something wrong with my make-up. I guessed He had more important things to do as of course they have remained blue, though my hair is no longer black.

Our day at the Home began at 7.30. Beds in the big dormitory had to be left tidy and stripped back to air; the older girls who slept in the small balcony room tended to be less careful as their beds were not so easily seen by those in authority. Everyone had to be washed, dressed, hair brushed and all other toilet arrangements completed before going down to breakfast in the schoolroom. This was served at 8.00 o'clock. Breakfast was usually a few slices of bread and margarine, or sometimes a bowl of bread and milk or lumpy porridge in cold weather. Though we sometimes felt the amount was rather small and the quality poor, we did have three good meals a day.

Girls too young to attend school were taught at home by older girls who had left school at the age of fourteen. There were usually about twelve of us between the ages of five and fourteen who attended St. Peter's School in Lower Parkstone; this was a Church school belonging to St. Peter's Church just across the road. About one hundred and fifty children attended the school.

We walked the mile to school four times a day. As we went down the steep hill, two by two in a crocodile, we were fearful that the brakes of the trams would fail as they hurtled down the hill. Woe betide any girl who became too venturesome or frivolous: some unseen watcher would report unseemly behaviour such as breaking ranks to pick a flower, having a quick run up an inviting slope or playfully pushing or slapping one another. Then we would face a severe lecture in the evening on correct behaviour.

One incident leaps from the dimness of memory. It happened one winter morning when the roads and paths were icy. I slipped and fell, cutting my knee badly. One of the older girls used a hanky to tie the bleeding wound and rather than delay our arrival at school I struggled on - but not before going back a pace or two to look for the lost chip of flesh. When we reached school the teacher suggested I should be taken home to see a doctor: no nurses were in attendance at the school and telephones were unheard of, so it meant a long walk uphill to St. Faiths.

I expected a reprimand for going back early; by then the pain was getting severe and making me feel queer. Matron soon saw that I was not 'acting up' and I was put to bed. The doctor was sent for; I was not very alert when he came to look at the damage. As he walked away with matron I heard her say, 'One thing, doctor, she is not chicken-hearted.' I had no idea what she meant. The wound eventually healed; I still have a dimple in my knee.

St. Peter's followed the usual pattern of schools of this period: cold, dismal rooms, windows too high to look out of with only sky and clouds and an occasional bird visible. The toilet arrangements do not bear thinking about. The ones at the Home were nothing special but the school ones - ugh - I had to be desperate to use them. Some girls would sneak a quick look behind the boy's partition and reported that their arrangements were even worse. Even then the school was condemned but it is still in use today although it is no longer connected financially to the church.

In the infant's classroom were large glossy pictures of the four seasons: spring had lambs and calves, flowers and fields with trees; summer showed trees heavy with deeper greens and a blue haze above; autumn - full of golden, red colours and trees less burdened, with their leaves scattered on the ground; and winter showed a shepherd carrying a lamb in his arm, a dog by his side and sheep huddled in snow and pale sunshine reflected in frozen cart-tracks.

We left the Infants when we were six, to go to the Juniors. There were more classes there and each teacher remained with the same class most of the time, although for needlework and singing those teachers best at those particular subjects took over. My least favourite lesson was arithmetic: even today rows of figures make my mind clam up - and I cannot enjoy them. Geography, history and singing were just about tolerated; reading, writing, sewing and recitation I enjoyed: possibly I showed off a bit with them as they were my favourite subjects.

We had to wear a uniform to school which meant that we could always be recognised. One of the garments we disliked was the scarlet woollen cape which had a hood bound with black silky braid and fastened with large buttons. If only we had appreciated the comfort they provided, protecting us all through the winter months as we trudged to and from school. Feminine pride blinded us to this aspect and we felt that they set us apart from other school girls who teased us. We could be seen from a long distance processing along the roads and the other girls would chant: 'Here come the Home girls', which upset us. Sometimes boys joined in and chucked things at us: we dared not retaliate unless a bold girl stuck her tongue out. It never seemed to occur to grown ups that our identifying clothes could possibly cause children mental distress. I know that there were many excellent and practical reasons for having uniforms but children do not always use logic for things they like or dislike. These garments had been donated years before my time by a generous and thoughtful benefactor and they were handed down from one girl to another for years.

Equally unflattering, we felt, were our summer pinafores: bright red with small white spots, which were worn to protect our red, white and blue-striped galatea dresses. But the garments I remember most clearly were summer dresses of rather stiff material in a crushed strawberry colour, with short bodices edged with white feather-stitching - handsewn which made our fingers sore. Nearly all our clothes were made by the girls under strict supervision of matron who was an excellent teacher. Most of the clothes were sewn on a machine but any fancy stitching, button holes and hems had to be done by hand during the evening sewing hour. The older girls had summer dresses made of softer, lighter material called nain-sook; the bodices were more tight-fitting and the flared, long skirts fell in pretty folds and had short sleeves. This dainty effect was spoilt by the rather drab, almost khaki-coloured material.

We wore uncomfortable straw boaters which either fitted too tightly on the side of one's head or were too loose and wobbled as we walked. We had to embroider, in yellow silk, the motif 'S.F.' onto small squares of scarlet-corded ribbon which was then sewn onto the black ribbon band. That job was even worse than sewing galatea: many a pricked finger left its smear of blood inside the hat - and you can imagine what other girls called us with such initials so boldly displayed.

Our winter dresses were made of heavy navy-blue serge bought by the bolt from wholesalers in Portsmouth at a spe-cial price; we were told it was the same material that was used for sailors' uniforms in the Royal Navy. I doubt if they had red feather-stitching on their cuffs and collars like we did, to enliven the dark-blue colour. Our winter pinafores were made of stiff gaberdine with pinstripes in red-and-white on a dark-blue material.

For outdoors we wore long navy-blue coats and flat tam-o'-shanter hats which we called pancakes. Miss Langley always inspected us before we set out; after this they had a tenden-cy to tilt and slant to suit the wearer's fancy.

On Sundays we wore different clothes and we wore shoes instead of our sturdy school boots. No pinafores adorned our best dresses although the tiny ones wore pretty white ones indoors, tucked and embroidered with short frilly sleeves looking like gay butterflies.

Our footwear almost needs a chapter to itself. Through the kind action of a benefactor each girl was provided annually with one pair of boots known as 'clod-hoppers' and one pair of shoes. A special arrangement was made with a local shoe shop for us to be the only customers on two successive Saturday afternoons - the shop was closed to anyone else requiring footwear for that time. I marvel at the patience of the staff who coaxed and fitted shoes and boots on so many pairs of different feet. We all wore thick hand-knitted woollen black socks or stockings which slid and wrinkled as shoes and boots were changed. Often the would-be wearer was in tears before satisfaction was achieved. Even though they had thick soles and heavy uppers, at least the shoes were new; but we were not allowed the pleasure of gloating over our new footwear or the pleasure of trying them on again: every pair was put into a special cupboard, locked and not used until the following year; last year's choosing became the next year's wearing. It was explained to us that this was more economical - but I have still not worked out the logic of it.

When necessary our footwear was repaired by a man who lived in a terraced cottage on the way to Newton, who called regularly at the Home. It was impressed on us that we should never look down-at-heel, which was a mark of poverty. It was also considered poverty-stricken to show where a garment had been mended: in those days patches and darns had to be almost invisible.

We must have carried a fair weight in the amount of garments that were piled on our young bodies. The precept of always wearing wool next to the skin meant woollen vests. These were a source of discomfort to girls with sensitive skin and were called 'scratchy and itchy vests'.

This was covered by a cotton or flannelette chemise. Any girl who had a weak chest and was liable to colds in the winter had to wear a chest protector. This was a piece of flannel or coarse brown paper shaped like a bib at the back and front and slipped over the head. During cold and foggy weather it would be smeared with goose-grease, made from the Christmas bird, or if none was available, lard was used: in those days there would always be a bladder of lard kept for this and culinary purposes.

Next, stays or a bodice were worn,the latter made of two layers of flannel stitched criss-cross fashion to hold them together, with buttons at each side to hold our drawers up.

We wore two pairs of drawers: one made of cotton worn as a lining and more easily washed than our navy bloomers; there was a band around the waist with button holes in it which corresponded with buttons on the bodice. Woe betide any girl whose buttons were not firmly fixed; bending and stretching exercises would result in the buttons popping off suddenly. Then the consequences would be most embarrassing: if only one side-button gave way the bloomer leg would slide down and show beneath the hem of one's dress; but if two went the navy bloomers descended to lie in a heap around one's feet. This usually happened while the school were having Drill. If it was possible, the unfortunate girl would step out of the garment and stuff it inside the white lining drawers. Or we would try to hide them and ask to 'be excused' and make a hasty exit to the toilet. At the Home, matron would chide the careless girl and say, 'You sewed that on with a hot needle and burning thread.'

Our stays had tapes which had to be tied to loops sewn at the top of our stockings to keep them up. Sometimes the tapes would come adrift and hang down the front of one's leg, bobbing merrily, if untidily, as we played games at school or home. Hankies also had to have a loop in one corner and be tied on, making it almost impossible to reach in time of need. More often, the hanky would be tucked into a sleeve. Why we had no pockets I cannot imagine. Next we wore one or two petticoats according to the season. And over all this a dress, and a pinafore for indoors, although we often wore them over dresses for school.

We knew little about 'women's pains', as menstruation was genteely described in those days. We were never told about it directly. During our sewing hour in the evenings, girls who were not very good at needlework were given squares made from old sheets; these were folded and seamed all round: two diagonal corners had small loops of tape sewn across. We were told these were 'white dusters'. When a girl remarked that she had never seen them used, there was a hush and the subject changed. These were to be sanitary towels. If a girl had started her periods while still at St. Faiths, the soiled articles were put into a pail of cold water and covered. The owner had then to wash them clean after school. They were put to dry in a discreet corner of the outside wash-house, never displayed on lines in the back yard. Each girl was given six of these squares and told, 'You will know what they are for when your time comes.' My own time did not come until I had left to go into service at Lilliput. What a shock I had then. I thought I must have done something wicked and was being punished. The housemaid enlightened me into the mysteries of Womanhood. I was almost seventeen then.

Discipline at the Home was very strict in all matters; lies and deceit were never tolerated. Whatever we had done wrong, punishment was more lenient if we owned up and spoke the truth. Honesty became our watchword.

Some of the things not allowed were: talking during meals or after we were in bed; accepting gifts from other schoolgirls or visiting them at their homes; going out alone and certainly, never after dark. And very important - we were not to talk to boys and never, no never, accept sweets or gifts from them. If we met a gentleman whom we recognised, we must not converse with him unless accompanied by an adult from St. Faiths. On Sundays we were not allowed to sew, knit or play with dolls or other toys. We were expected, instead, to sing hymns, read good books and write 'thank you' letters.

Before evening prayers a slate was produced which recorded our marks for the day. Each name was set down and a good or bad mark was set beside it: a tick or a cross, and for each misdemeanour a good mark was lost. At the end of the week those children with bad marks had to forfeit the one sweet we were given as a reward for good behaviour. How that slate pencil would squeak as it listed the day's doings. On Saturday night the slate was wiped clean again.

One frequent punishment was to be sent to bed with dry bread and cold water. Sometimes this punishment was made bearable if a friend smuggled in something more tasty such as a scrap of bread with a scrape of marge or smear of jam on it, to be eaten in secret with guilty enjoyment.

Another punishment was to make the culprit stand in a corner facing a blank wall for half-an-hour or so, or until an apology was given. Punishment corner was near the foot of the stairs, almost opposite the schoolroom door and there was a blank drab green wall to look at. Even a stray spider would have added interest, although for some girls this would have brought terror. (Few spiders could have eluded the frequently wielded brushes of the household brigade.) Occasionally one was seen, or worse, one touched an arm or leg; the reaction was always a terrified scream: it is one thing to watch a spider in bright sunlight spinning a delicate web of fine gossamer sparkling with dewdrops, but quite another matter to feel one without seeing it clearly. This added considerably to a child's punishment - a spider became a sinister creature and the fear could be great in a highly-strung childish imagination. Not all girls suffered so much, some took it in their stride and generally speaking, punishment for breaking the rules or being extra naughty would be accepted as just and deserved.

I was probably about ten when I was tempted and fell: the devil is very crafty. One day I had to go through to Miss Langley's part of the house to deliver a message. To reach it I had to pass through the vestibule, usually called 'best o' view' by us girls. It had a glazed front door, with coloured glass designs in some of the panes and a tiled floor. An odd dark polished table stood by the inner wall; on it was placed a dish of luscious desert plums - they were a golden-red, with a delicious smell of ripeness, enough to make one's mouth water. I stood with no evil thought at first, just enjoying the loveliness of the colouring. 'Go on, one will not be missed' said the tempter, 'taste and try'. I did. Hiding one under my pinny, I crept to the blank side of the house along the almost unused mossy pathway and ate the stolen fruit. Oh, it was sweet. I threw the stone into the shrubbery and went back indoors to deliver the message and left rather quickly: I felt sure I must have looked guilty.

Conscience would not let me forget my 'crime'; even one plum stolen was wrong. After evening prayers I managed to waylay Miss Langley in the vestibule and told her of my shame and sin. Gently she chided me for stealing but her eyes did not condemn me. No doubt in her wisdom she realised that I had suffered. My punishment was light: I was bidden to ask our Heavenly Father to forgive me and not to let the other girls know of my weak moment. I was told to pray for strength to resist any temptation in future. You may be sure I had learnt my lesson.

At school, a favourite ploy of teachers was to punish a pupil by making him or her stand on a form for several minutes with hands clasped on top of the head. Until you have tried standing like this for even a few minutes you can have no idea of the effect. It was not only demoralising - to be the object of scorn, pity or ridicule of the rest of the class - but it caused sheer physical exhaustion and some girls actually fainted, providing a diversion for the rest of the class.

We had plenty of religious instruction in our lives. Miss Langley would read to us from the Bible and we had to learn verses from the Psalms, hymns and the Christian Year by John Keble; also the Collect of the week from the Prayer Book.

Any girl who had not been baptised before coming to St. Faiths was christened at a private ceremony and always took Faith as a second name. As each of us reached a suitable age we were prepared for confirmation by the Bishop of Salisbury.

Louie and I were ready in 1918, the year of the 'flu epidemic. Our confirmation had to be postponed for several weeks until Advent Sunday and we took our first Communion on Christmas Day. To mark the occasion we were presented with a special book about the Holy Communion and the way to prepare oneself for this solemn ceremony.

We attended St. Peter's Church every Sunday for matins; we sat in a separate part of the church at the side of the pulpit, in view of most of the congregation. Often compliments were passed to matron or Miss Langley about our attention during the service, or our singing and knowledge of the hymns and psalms. After Sunday School in the afternoon we went to the Children's service; then we sat with all the other girls and looked different only because of our short hair and darker clothes. During the light summer evenings we would go to Evensong if we wished; we liked to go, often with Miss Langley, as it was a break from routine and was not compulsory. We were allowed to walk in orderly groups rather than in formation and we sat in the main part of the church. As the procession from the vestry to the choir stalls passed our pews, I used to wonder how the small choir boys would be seen when they stood in the pulpit for I was under the misunderstanding that everyone took turns to preach. It was sometime before I realised that only the ones wearing certain robes were the clergymen, and the rest formed the choir. The first vicar I remember was Canon Heygate. He had a gentle wrinkled face with kindly eyes capable of twinkling when he talked to us on visits to the Home and school.

Sometimes, in the summer evenings, we would go to a different church, St. Clements at Newtown near Upper Parkstone; it was a fair distance to walk but it was more a treat than a duty. This was a country church with less ornate furnishings and ritual; we liked the homely atmosphere and the hymns seemed to be sung more lustily. I wished I could join in but I made a dreadful noise so I merely opened my mouth to form the words and let out no accompanying sound.

On our way home from this church we could, if we had been good, go to the viewpoint at the top of Constitution Hill and look right across Poole Harbour towards Sandbanks, seeing woods with houses nestling among them and Brownsea and other islands in the harbour.

St. Peter's was known as a High Church and I loved the ritual and rich colours of the robes worn to suit each season of the Christian year. Hymn 133 in the Ancient and Modern book calls Easter the 'Queen of Seasons.' As a girl I loved that phrase: it seemed so right for the happy spring festival. In the church's year each season has a distictive set of colours and I think that gold and green are the ones for Easter - light and delicate after the mourning purple and black of the Lenten period when every sacred ornament was shrouded in these sombre colours and the altar left bare of the cross and candles - while only the processional silver cross remained on the wall. Suddenly, gone are gloom and doom; welcome as the first rays of warming spring sunshine, were the daffodils, jonquils and other flowers with their tender green foliage once more adorning the spotless white cloth on the High Altar. Out came the banners, brushed and dusted in readiness for the Easter Sunday procession. In childhood days I never gave a thought to the skill and patience of the people who made and cared for these beautifully embroidered banners. To us they were a familiar part of the mysterious ritual of the Christian year.

Springtime colours of gold, white and green were enhanced by the sunshine streaming through the stained glass windows. Girls who had been confirmed attended the first early Service of Holy Communion on Easter Sunday at 6.30. No food was allowed before partaking of the Sacrament. When I was old enough I felt I was 'set apart' for that day. We had walked to the church and sometimes it could be quite chilly at that time of the morning but to us it was not a duty, but a privilege, to attend this Sung Eucharist, which I thought was a lovely name. The beauty and solemnity of this awe inspiring service was enriched by the singing of hymns and anthems by the choir: it gave one a special kind of feeling that lasted most of the day.

We looked forward to the Children's Service in the afternoon. The procession started after the first prayer had been said and one hymn sung: choir boys and men led the way, followed by some of the clergy and then those of the congregation who wished to do so; banners were carried at intervals. I longed to carry one in the procession but I had no realisation of their heavy weight. Being small for my age I was only allowed to hold one of the tasselled cords at the side which were intended to prevent the banner from twisting sideways, while a taller girl carried it proudly aloft. Right through the church we processed, even passing into the dim mysterious passage behind the altar which never seemd to be used on any other occasion; it smelt dusty and damp and made one shiver. To my mind this place symbolised the weeks of Lent and the dank, dark sacred tomb. The emergence into the bright sunlight outside was a symbol of breaking the bonds of death and the resurrection: perhaps this was intentional.

The long procession headed by the now unshrouded and gleaming silver cross on its ebony staff, garlanded with spring flowers, wended its way all round the churchyard. Hymns were sung - the ones with the most verses and the men's voices blending with the choir boys' clear trebles. The large jewelled ring worn by the vicar fascinated us: it seemed to us a peculiar idea as men in ordinary life did not wear rings or jewellery. We did not know its Ecclesiastical significance then. The clergy also wore heavy robes, richly patterned and embroidered in wonderful colours and designs. Joyfully we walked along exulting at being part of this glad ceremony. Gradually we made our way down the short road, passing St. Peter's school: how full of importance we felt when we caught a glimpse of a familiar face among those lining the road. Somehow it always seemed bright and sunny. Everything glistened and gleamed; the sun's rays filtered down in silent benediction through the fresh green leaves of the newly-awakened trees while the dark yews in the churchyard made a sombre background.

We girls really loved these events and felt a slight pang of unwillingness to re-enter the building for the final hymn and blessing. If only I could have joined in the singing my joy would have been complete - but only the Creator could hear my inward hymn of praise: spiritually I was uplifted with holy joy of Easter - the Queen of seasons.

During the six weeks of Lent, no sweets were allowed. On Easter Sunday any girl lucky enough to have lost no marks received a large solid block of chocolate with whole nuts in as a reward: this was called 'hobnails'. Anyone with a few bad marks was given a smaller block or some sweets, and the little ones were given a cute fluffy-yellow chick with an Easter egg; no girl went without some prize.

Helping to decorate the church was one of the highlights of our young days. At Newton we helped in the rewarding task of preparing for Easter and Harvest Thanksgiving. At Harvest time people brought all their garden produce in wheelbarrows, on handcarts, bikes or in bags of all sizes and shapes: not many folk had cars in those days. Among the gifts were massive marrows and huge round pumkins which we could not lift and were gently scolded for trying to roll one along the aisle. Mounds of beans - long and bumpy, scrubbed potatoes, gleaming carrots, lengthy parsnips, beetroot which had to be handled with care to prevent from bleeding, white and peachy-coloured turnips and cabbages with hard, shiny hearts - almost too big for us to carry, beautiful green apples and ruddy-gold pears which could have nothing put on top of them in case they bruised. We even saw exotic-looking grapes and were allowed to eat one or two if they came off the bunch - but not inside the church. I had the distinction of possessing an attractively shaped basket which was used for the grapes. It was lined with pretty leaves and carefully filled with the luscious fruit: purple grapes having a lovely bloom and pale transluscent green ones looking as if they had trapped an atom of sunshine inside their skins, like sunbeams under water. This was put in a special place on the altar. I kept that basket for years; it seemed to have a special aura of its own - it was one of my treasures.

Every nook and corner of the church had something to dress it up, even the pillars were draped in lovely 'tingly-tangly' smelling hop vines - though these wilted before the Harvest Festival was really over. There were special Harvest loaves in the design of a sheaf of corn or a long twisting plait with a crispy top crust which was rather tough when we finally came to eat it several days later. A sheaf of real corn stood at the head of the aisle. Once, in the middle of a service, a tiny mouse peeped out, unnoticed by most people. Flowers in profusion were arranged everywhere: gaudy dahlias adorned the window-sills catching the evening sunlight, and glowing ever more brightly, michaelmas daisies were placed at the base of pillars and Canterbury bells proclaimed the wonderful works of the Creator. More trailing hops hung below the pulpit and I can only hope the preacher enjoyed their distinctive smell as much as I did. It is many years since I went to a real country Harvest Thanksgiving Service: I wonder if it would still seem as wonderful as it did in those days.

On the day following Harvest Sunday, we had the pleasant task of bearing away many of the spoils as we were among those chosen to receive the bounties of the earth. For days, we truly did live on the fat of the land in contrast to our usual diet, which though adequate, was a bit monotonous. Although the bread was stale no other loaf tasted quite like it; perhaps we imagined it or thought it had been doubly blest with a flavour of its own. I think we even had real butter on it. We did not carry all the produce home from the church ourselves. Kindly people would bring the heavier things but some girls were chosen to bring the apples or some other edible items and naturally they did not always hurry back - what matter if an apple or two or even a well-scrubbed carrot did not reach its true destination.

Marrows and pumpkins were stored in the cupboard under the stairs, on rather high shelves; many a pound of marrow and pumkin, or marrow and apple jam was made to store for the winter. The huge cabbages with hard green hearts, carrots, parsnips, beet and turnips were put on the floor until the door would barely shut. Rather floppy lettuces and limp red-and-white radishes were put in bowls of water to crisp them up, then they were stood on the cool stone pantry floor. The grapes I think were sent to local hospitals although Miss Langley may have had some for herself and her sister. Perishable items all added variety to our normal diet.

I have a vivid recollection of a 'new' vegetable being included called sugar-beet which we had never known before. Not surprisingly, we wanted to sample such a sweetly named specimen but were disappointed when our teeth met on stringy flesh with a really horrible taste. I can still recall it, but how can taste be described when it is not what one expects or when it has never been known before or since. It certainly had no flavour of sugar or sweetness. Perhaps it served as a punishment for our greed. We did not know that it had to go through many processes before it became sugar.

At Christmas too the church looked beautiful; bright lights in the winter gloom, silvery stars, lovely flowers and carol singing all made a deep and lasting impression on us. Memory holds a picture of the seven chased-silver lamps with glowing ruby lights in the heart of each one, hanging in the sanctuary. Around the massive pillars where fixed wreaths of evergreens; I often wondered how they were fixed so that they did not slip down.

Christmas really started for us about a fortnight before the actual day: this was called Parcel Time because all kinds of parcels would arrive by post or other messengers. Our season lasted until well after Christmas with parties, pantomine visits and our own concert nights when we performed plays and charged a fee to help with finances. We had a Punch and Judy show once and another time a lady gave us a party at her house and we heard a gramophone playing music.

In those days the postman used to call at odd times, sometimes in the evenings; he would get used to seeing a row of eager faces peering out of the window and he would give us a cheery greeting. We were not allowed to answer the front door and all parcels were spirited away: we never discovered where they were hidden. On Christmas Day, any presents sent to individual children were piled on a table for the lucky owners who shared the contents with less fortunate ones.

St. Faiths had many kind benefactors and friends, who were always included in our prayers each evening and so at Christmas we received a considerable portion of goodwill. We received several regular and very welcome gifts: one of the best remembered were three casks of hand-picked and individually wrapped apples, all rosy and shining in tissue paper. They were ordered at harvest time and kept for us until Christmas - a very generous gift from a kind-hearted lady. Two or three large cakes, rich and fruity with marzipan and icing concealing the richness within, usually arrived from different sources. Oranges in crates, some with silver paper showing between the wooden slats, were glimpsed as they stood awhile in the passage; boxes of crackers and biscuits with pretty designs on the tins were whisked out of sight until Christmas Eve. Authority was probably too busy to take much notice of our sly sallies to see anything new that had arrived. Discipline was relaxed somewhat and authority was a little blind at times.

One lady, whose name was never revealed to us, gave every child a gift. After prayers one day early in November, a list was handed round and each child wrote down what she would like: generally books, writing cases complete with stationary, pencil or needlework boxes, each fitted out with appropriate things inside.

Puddings, mincemeat and fuit cakes had been made much earlier in November; even the tiniest children had a traditional 'stir and wish'. A few days were set aside before Christmas Eve for making the decorations for the school room. Most girls preferred making the gaily coloured chains and rosettes of vivid colours rather than the difficult task of threading holly. This was left to the older girls who were provided with gloves and scissors, strong needles and stout thread for the job. Leaves were stripped off the branches and every leaf threaded separately and pressed on top of the last one until there was enough to make a garland long enough to frame the recessed windows above the mantleshelf over the stove. Varicoloured large rosettes of paper were attached at intervals and the whole thing hung up on the green distempered wall. It was very effective and distinctive and repaid those girls whose fingers became sore with the task. I have never seen this form of decoration since. Inside the rosettes were placed my favourite decoration: a large shiny red-and-gold man-in-the-moon, perpetual smiling from his place of honour; he was flanked by two big royal-blue glass balls; other places were brightned with red-and-gold balls, and sprigs of holly and ivy were placed wherever there was an empty space around the walls.

Naturally, we had a Christmas tree, brought to the door by a sad-faced man who drove us to Sandbanks. The tree remained out of sight until Chrismas Eve when it was put in a corner of the school room, hidden by a screen of black American cloth covered with ancient and well-loved cards and scraps. Gifts were not hung on the tree but piled around the base, each bearing a child's name and Miss Langley would distribute them on the evening of Christmas Day. Real candles in small holders would be clipped onto the branches but not lit until the last minute. A strict watch was kept on the candle flames and a bucket of water and one of sand kept ready just in case of mishap.

The evening of Christmas Eve was really exciting: the kitchen, where loitering was usually forbidden, was open to all, and the tinies were allowed to stay up later than usual, probably in the hope that they would go to sleep more quickly once they were tucked up in bed. To keep the rest of us out of the way while the school room was being transformed, carols were sung and last minute homemade gifts finished. At intervals the door would open a few inches and an apple or orange would roll across the floor, sent in by an unseen hand, until each girl had something. It was a point of honour not to peep to see whose hand might be doing the rolling. Still in the warm kitchen, with the cosy glow of the fire, it was time for prayers and the Bible story of the first Christmas was read, then off to bed.

The day dawned at last. It began with the eldest girls going off in the chilly darkness to Holy Communion at 6.30 while those at home helped the excited little ones to dress and prevent anyone creeping down to have a peep in the school room. By 8.30 even the youngest and slowest girl would be dressed and waiting for the bell to ring, summoning us down. By tradition the youngest went first and although it was Christmas Day we had to descend the stairs two by two and no pushing. Cries of joy and squeals of delight greeted the transformation of our dingy room to a hall of grandeur. The lights were kept on although it was daytime and the long table was covered by a gleaming white cloth which was almost hidden under piles of gifts; down the centre were heaps of apples, oranges and nuts and crackers and festive hats which were saved for later in the day.

It is hard to describe the next hour but easy to imagine. Gradually order was restored, grace was said and breakfast started. Afterwards the girls who had already been to church stayed to help prepare dinner, the rest went to Matins and enjoyed the sight of the decorated church, the carols and cheery greeting from well-wishers.

Dinner was a real Christmas Feast consisting usually of a large goose with all the trimmings, donated every year by a benefactor. It must have been a work of art to prepare the vegetables, stuffing, gravy and the bird itself. The tinies had chicken, I think, as goose is a very rich meat. During the meal we were allowed to talk but I doubt if we stopped feeding to say much until the huge pudding was ceremoniously brought in, topped with real sparklers sending out showers of silvery sparks with gay abandon. Then the silence was broken with exclamations of wonder at this delight: no one was really impatient to be served with the rich pudding until every spark had died out. The pudding also hid the secrets of the time-honoured charms - all real silver, and even though the lucky girls had to hand back the charms they found it did not lessen the excitement in searching for hidden treasure. A ring signified forthcoming marriage or romance, silver coins for wealth, a thimble for a spinster - but why a button for a bachelor was included is anyone's guess. Care had to be taken to make sure that none of these would disappear down a little 'red lane' or in more prosaic terms, get swallowed. On that special day we sang our grace: 'Be present at our table Lord, be here and everwhere adored, these creatures bless and grant that we may feast in Paradise with Thee.' At the end of the meal we said 'Thank you God for our good dinner' - and I doubt if any of us could have eaten another mouthful.

Some of the little ones were encouraged to rest after such a large meal, middle girls went for a walk - not a very popular suggestion; older girls who had helped with the dinner were detailed to clear away and wash up. Then there were plenty of presents to look at again as we had only had time for a quick look earlier in the day.

The afternoon passed with various activities until tea-time: thin bread and butter tempted our appetites. Large iced cakes were on show and never cut on Christmas Day but kept until our concert nights; small cakes satisfied us well. To me the best things were the delicate china cups, saucers and plates which were kept for special occasions: so dainty we were almost afraid to handle them; the inner pleasure they gave us lingers with me still. Only the eldest girls were allowed to clear away and wash them up; then they were packed away in tissue paper until the next occasion.

The evening was a real highlight; screens were moved away from the small tree and the coloured candles were lit. The doors of the stove were left open giving a warm glow; this made a lovely setting for carol singing. Miss Langley, who was no mere figurehead but entered a great deal into our lives, handed out every gift with a special kiss for the little ones; and for the older girls a blessing and a much cherished word of praise. Matron looked less severe than usual; she too had many gifts and I often wonder where some of the less well-made things finished their lives. Even Roy, the dog, had a gift-wrapped bone and dear Miss Nina joined in for a while.

After the little ones had gone to bed with a new toy allowed just for once, the older girls had their own special hallowed hour when favouite carols were beautifully sung. Two of Miss Langley's favourites were 'In the fields with their flocks abiding; and 'The stars are shining bright and clear' - a lovely carol telling a story and building a Christmas word picture. Gradually girls would silently disappear until only a few of us were left sitting in the light from the fire and a small lamp. Then suddenly the lights would go up again and Miss Langley received the special gift which the girls had saved up for. One year she was given a beautiful soft fur coat; she was speechless when it was handed to her by Nellie and the oldest girl. We all felt it was a really hallowed and magic moment.

Prayers ended the day and 'God bless our benefactors and friends' was said with more fervour than usual. Sincerity and gratitude to Miss Langley and the others was humbly shown as we sang an evening hymn. And then to bed.

Several ideas and methods were used to boost the funds of the Home: sales of work, an annual Pound Day, concerts at Christmas and the highlight of the year for us - Anniversary Day, when all the benefactors and friends came to see what progress each girl was making.

We also collected from nearby houses and were allowed to do so in the evenings. I enjoyed going round in pairs and seeing the homes of rich people but I hated the idea of asking for something for nothing. But I think it was the warm bright well-appointed kitchens which planted the idea in my head that I would like to be a cook. These people were very kind to us and played a large part in our lives. We did not always know the measure of their generosity: some paid an annual sum of money; some donated gifts in kind and some probably spent time doing things for us. Clothes which were no longer fashionable yet not worn out gave much pleasure to any girl lucky enough to benefit. Fruit and vegetables from their gardens made very acceptable gifts; treats and outings in the school holidays and presents at Christmas time all helped to swell the funds in one way or another. One of our benefactors would send baskets of strawberries which were a real treat - even without cream.

The first of May was Pound Day; we girls welcomed any interruption of routine and enjoyed the activity and excitement which Pound Day brought with it. About a week in advance hand-written notices of the event were delivered to houses over a known locality. The wording went like this: 'The annual Pound day at St. Faiths Home will be held on May 1st. All contributions will be thankfully received and gratefully acknowledged.'

On the first of May, the schoolroom furniture was

rearranged. Girls who had left school were put in charge of a section where they would receive pounds of jam, marmalade, bottled fruit and vegetables. Another section would house piles of dried goods: peas, lentils, rice, barley, flour and such like, all accumulated and brought by faithful benefactors and friends. Sometimes jars or boxes of sweets were donated. Very few people came with only one pound of this or that and these supplies enriched the store cupboard by no small degree. Cakes and buns and other teatime fancies were received with glee, adding interest to our bread and marge diet. Miss Grainge and Dorothy collected cash and excitement mounted as the day wore on and piles grew and spread.

During the 1914-18 War we still held our Pound Days. Donations may have been less but the generous spirits still prevailed. After the day was over we neatly wrote notes which we took to each house whose kindly donor had added to our stores.

Prize giving days were held in October to celebrate the start of St. Faiths. The second Thursday in the month marked the anniversary and was always known as the 'Anni'. Many benefactors and friends came to look at conditions and see some of our work. They would suggest possible improvements or alterations, make speeches and present prizes. The older girls sang hymns or gave recitations: the little ones did anything they fancied to impress the honoured guests. To us, the Anni was a red-letter day, a lovely humble-jumble: everything different. We wore our best clothes, had better food, extra cake, very thin bread and butter - not the usual doorsteps of bread and marge, and lemonade to drink.

Miss Langley's birthday was another occasion for celebration. It was a custom on that day to greet her in French as she came into the schoolroom for morning prayers. We began, 'Bonjour, mademoiselle'; I do not remember the whole phrase but the end - 'Heigh ho, mademoiselle' always made me want to giggle: it seemed such an odd thing to say to a very mature lady.

St. Faiths had its own sale-of-work held in December. During the year any girls who could knit, sew, crochet, paint, draw or make anything saleable would be encouraged to do so and there would be quite a variety of goods produced. We knitted bed socks, hug-me-tights (a snug-fitting garment like a jumper with low neckline and no sleeves), wristlets, scarves, shawls and crossovers (a kind of shawl which was crossed over the body and the ends tied in the front). I remember Miss Grainge making cord-sashes of silk strands: several strands were divided into two or three lots, as for plaiting; one end was tied to a door handle, the other held by a girl. The strands were twisted together tighter and tighter until the cord clung and looped with tension. As the hold was loosened, tension slackened. A towel or cloth was quickly rubbed the length of the cord until it held without kinking or unravelling. Some unusual things are brought to mind: we made tiny strawberry cushions in red velvet, with tiny yellow stitches to represent the seeds of the strawberry. They were filled with emery powder and were fitted into a dried beechmast case and used when sewing-needles became rusty or sticky. I also made little pen-wipers from scraps of cloth with a wishbone base. The head was made of black sealing wax stuck over wool, wound around the blade, and small white beads made the eyes and teeth. A hooked nose was essential; for this wax was pulled into shape while still warm. Blobs of sealing wax made the feet and the two sticks of bone dressed with black woollen material were the body and legs. Over this was put a red cloak and hood. A tiny strip of paper bore the words, written very small, 'Once I was a wishbone living in a hen. Now I'm just a little slave made to wipe your pen.' There were many other more ingenious but useless articles made for the sale such as cardboard boxes, 'dressed up' in delicate pale-coloured material, usually finished with spot-muslin frills all round. The top of the lid was padded to make a pincushion. If girls wished to keep what they had made, the article would be put on show and marked 'sold'. It was an exciting event especially for the older girls who helped on some of the stalls. It was open to the public and the benefactors and friends rallied around once more. It was a valiant effort on our part to swell the funds and all of us enjoyed it. In the evening we would have a special tea to celebrate the occasion.

Events

I was about eleven years old when I became an inmate of the Fever Hospital at Alderney. All cases of infectious diseases were sent there; I caught scarlet fever and was taken there in a black-painted van which we called the fever van. Diptheria and in some cases measles, were also classed as infectious illnesses; all cases were notifiable and the patient isolated. Strangely enough, I do not recall any of the other girls at the Home getting Scarlet Fever. I have little remembrance of how it started although I do remember that my throat was very sore and I was unusually hot.

On the first night in the hospital I was half asleep when I heard a strange voice say, 'Here's a new boy'; I thought I was dreaming but was conscious enough to say scornfully, 'I'm <u>not</u> a boy'. It seemed dreadful to be thought of as a boy but my hair was cropped short and I was almost smothered in blankets.

The period of isolation was six weeks and in all that time I did not have a single visitor. It stands to reason that no-one from St. Faiths could come and neither could my mother and sisters who all lived too far away.

At first visitors at the hospital could only see patients through a glass screen until the first period of isolation, lasting two weeks, was over. Any gifts of toys, books, puzzles and even dolls had to be left behind when the patient was well enough to leave the hospital. These were all I had to amuse me; I did not care for comics - my chief delight was reading books or looking at a large tin full of picture postcards. I felt sure visitors used to pity me and would invite their children to share their sweets or fruit with me. Although I enjoyed such gifts I did not have anything to give in return so I would make up stories and tell them in bed when we were tucked in for the night, as a gesture of thanks.

I remember a postcard my mother sent me while in the hospital, which was a view of Blackfriars Bridge in London. I felt a sense of disappointment that it was not gayer - but I was not aware of the difficult life she had to lead to keep herself and my two sisters.

When I was well enough to go out in the garden I liked to

wander around looking for flowers; I would ask the nurses if they knew their names but they did not always have time to tell me. One day two boys saw me on my own and said they had a new flower to show me. I went along with them and they led me to part of the garden I did not know. It was full of vegetables; they pulled up some carrots and swedes and wiped them on their trousers before starting to eat them. They dared me to join them and I was too frightened not to - they were much bigger than me. I was quite surprised at the taste of the swede. Scared as I was in case we were found out, I was flattered when they said I was a good sport. After that I tried to keep out of their way and I was not really sorry when they left the hospital before me. I quite enjoyed my stay there, and once the nurses found I could sew quite well, would do little jobs of sewing - putting tapes and loops on towels - it helped to fill the long days.

Recollections of seeing my mother and sisters together are vague as mother could not bring them often. When she could manage it she came by excursion train from London to Bournemouth and by tram to Parkstone. The trams stopped just outside the back gate. I must have been very young when they first came to visit me. My sisters both seemed pretty; I envied their summery cream dresses with wide sashes in blue ribbon, tied in a gorgeous bow at the back. My eldest sister, Churl, had blue eyes and fair hair, rippling in waves down her back: she looked like an angel. Ruby had deep hazel eyes and very dark hair and a lovely smile.

Some years later my mother came alone and an incident relating to that visit cast a shadow over my life. I had been told that my mother was coming to see me and had to fill the morning by playing in the quiet road - which we called 'up and down'. The woods were too wet on this particular day: we were all warned not to sit on the damp ground. In my state of suppressed excitement I rested on a heathery bank. That morning the hours seemed to crawl by; I could not put my heart into ordinary games and just waited in a state of tension for the call to say that my mother had arrived. I shall never know how my disobedience was discovered or who reported it. When I was told to go in, expecting to see mother, I was surprised to see only matron. Sternly she ordered me to go to the short passage leading to her sitting room. I wondered if my mother had been prevented from coming but instead I was told to learn some verses from the Psalms as a punishment. How could I concentrate? Miserably I tried but it was hopeless; not easily given to tears I swallowed hard and felt a wave of rebellion rise up inside me - and made no real attempt to learn the words. I admit I was sulky even when an older girl came to my rescue. She was supposed to hear me say my penalty piece but mumbled it through for me and reported that I had done it. I guess she could see how I felt. I was released and told to go and wash my face and hands and get ready to go out.

Presently, mother arrived; after kissing me she said, 'Edna looks very pale, Miss Grainge'. 'Yes', was her reply, 'I am sorry to tell you, Mrs Wright, that Edna has been a very naughty, disobedient girl and has had to be punished.'

Tears of shame, which I tried hard to keep back, pricked my eyes and almost brimmed over when mother said in a quiet voice, 'I am sure she is sorry, so can we go out now?'

Permission was given, and I had the thrill of riding on the upper deck of a tram into Bournemouth.

The events of the day are forgotten in detail but never can I forget or forgive the supidity of those in authority for the real anguish I suffered - not because of the punishment but because my mother was told in such harsh terms of a trifling misdemeanour. Even children have deep inner feelings.

I have a happier recollection of the time my mother came with my sisters and took us to Bournemouth and then by steamer to Swanage. To this day I refuse to believe that I was sea-sick; my sisters turned a funny colour almost as soon as we were on the water and I suppose that started me off too, but I attribute my sickness to the excitement of such a momentous occasion. A rare meeting, a ride on the open top-deck of a tram and a steamer trip, the sight of a sailor falling into the stream which flows through Bournemouth Pleasure Gardens, the wonder of seeing a huge sunflower -('It's bigger than my face' I told my mother) - what more could be needed to set up a physical reaction. And also the sense of unaccustomed freedom to be able to run and shout and laugh at all I saw. We three girls ran races but I was always last. Such events added variety to my childhood days. I did not very often think about the worries and anxieties and probable hardships of the lives of my mother and sisters in the days long before Social Security and help for one-parent families.

I always loved sewing and my efforts were considered good enough for me to try and enter a competition held by the Dorset Arts and Crafts Society. The garment chosen for me to make was a chemise which I had to sew completely by hand. There was more work in one such garment than several present-day dresses.

I had to do the actual cutting out under matron's supervision. Oh, the terror I felt as I held a huge pair of scissors and started to cut a sparkling white length of cotton material around the paper pattern which I had carefully pinned on top. I really trembled with tongue poking out between teeth in agony at every fresh snip: it seemed I was cutting out a tent. Matron, usually severe, was doing her best not to laugh outright but I was too anxious to notice this. Carefully I removed the pattern and matron said, 'Well, there's a lot of Jubilee Bumps along this side, so you must tidy that up.' Certainly the first side I had cut did look peculiar, though where the expression 'Jubilee Bumps' fitted in I was not sure.

Then it was ready to sew: each side had to be a 'run and fell' seam: that is, neat running stitches about half-an-inch from the edge, then pressed out flat and the whole length hemmed again. The front had an elaborate button and buttonhole strip; the left-side plain hemmed to take the buttons, the other piece put on to overlap for buttonholes and the bottom joined and the ends mitred to finish it off neatly. This strip went down about seven inches, not right to the bottom hem. Tucks were arranged to about the same depth, and the top fitted into a neck band without the slightest pucker; the bottom was hemmed all round. Calico is not the easiest material to sew and I dared not risk pricking a finger lest I leave a blood stain. Finally, the neckband, and front facing had to have a double row of feather-stitching and to make the job complete the button and buttonholes were done. Some secret tears were shed over this part as I was not too good at buttonhole stitching but, at last, it was finished. Matron allowed me to wash and iron it - another formidable process: not one of our present day, pre-set, plug-in, easy-to-use electric irons but a fairly weighty one heated on the kitchen range. Woe betide me, if I left the faintest smudge or scorch mark so, just to be on the safe side, I had started on a second garment. Eventually, my work was well and truly examined stitch by stitch and every part keenly looked over. Joy, oh joy, it passed scrutiny and was considered just about the standard to be entered for the exhibitiopn. Forms had to be filled in, with age, name and address, a guarantee to state that it was 'all my own work' and then the precious garment was duly wrapped in tissue paper and carried very carefully to the hall in Lower Parkstone, with other girls who had entered their work. They were exhibiting fine crochet, lace or knitting, all spread out with care and tacked on to pale blue paper to show it to the best advantage. It was the fashion to have collar and cuff sets in crochet work, exquisitely fine and delicate in design. Engrossed as I was with my own effort I am ashamed to say I did not realise how dainty and intricate this work was until I saw it on display. My only excuse is that I was the youngest one to enter anything. All exhibitors were allowed to go in free.

It was the first exhibition I had attended. Such a seemingly large hall, so many classes and bewildering display of Arts and Crafts to see: I could hardly bear to go across to the junior section marked 'under eleven years'. There, in the rather forlorn company of only one other exhibit - a carving by a boy - was my pathetic looking 'shimmy' beside a notice bearing the words, 'Not sufficient entries in this section to merit an award'. Not even a word of encouragement to children who had tried to make something by their own efforts.

I was a stolid, serious child and I guess this was the only reason that I did not throw a tantrum or run weeping from the hall in my disappointment. The lack of understanding shown by the judges, the callousness of not awarding some kind of consolation prize for entering anything at all, hit me; I fought back tears and went to join the others but my interest in the rest of the exhibition was shattered. Naturally they tried to comfort me, even teased me saying the judges did not know what it was supposed to be; some gave me sweets to console me but to this day I cannot forget the lack of commonsense shown by the organisers and officials. It was many years before I again attempted to show any work at exhibitions.

A small exhibition of Japanese work was brought to St. Faiths when I was about ten years old. It is a memory worth sharing: one day we had a feeling something unusual was about to happen, we could feel it in the air. In the middle of the day we had an extra wash and brush-up and were told to wear our Sunday dresses. During the afternoon a space was cleared in the schoolroom and to end our suspense, Miss Langley came in; she had with her a small lady whom we were told had come from a country far away, called Japan. She was a missionary who had spent much time there and dressed in Japanese fashion.

The older girls were asked to set out some tables and we were invited to sit cross-legged in a circle on the floor. Tiny frail china cups, saucers and plates were placed on the tables and a larger plate piled with miniature squares of cake no bigger than a sugar knob. Pale tea without milk or sugar was poured into doll-sized cups and offered to us with tiny cakes. Though not very satisfying they really melted in our mouths. We thought these cakes fit for a fairy feast: we were used to chunks, on the rare occasions when we had cake at all. We were not too sure about the tea but good manners and lack of a place to hide it prevented us from spitting it out or pouring it away. We were too polite to make any remark about it though I think the lady knew what we were thinking.

We were shown large pictures which had to be unrolled: two girls held the corners while they were explained to us. Mostly they were of the loveliness of the country: cherry blossom, festival days and things made in Japan. She had brought a few with her: delicate basket work and lengths of wonderfully fine silk and we were told about silkworms. It was hard for us to understand the miracle of this, how a caterpillar could spin anything so sheer and lovely to touch. She left us one picture which was later put up in the school room. It was a print of Christ in a white flowing robe with children of many nations around His feet: an ideal picture which we all liked. We did not really appreciate the designs on china and glass because we did not know anything about Japanese forms of art. Looking back it seems incredible that a nation with such delicate ideas, able to create beautiful things, could perpetrate the horrors and tortures which took place during the war in the East.

I remember many humorous incidents which enlivened our calls to local people. One in particular gives me a mental chuckle whenever it creeps into my mind. In our quest for donations, Louie and I toiled up a long winding pathway to a big house halfway up a hill. A lady, who was anything but slender was sitting outside in a deck chair and called to us as we hesitated, wondering which path to take. Obediently we approached her; as she rose the chair clung tightly to her 'sit-upon' - as we inelegantly called our posteriors. Not sure whether to proceed, retreat or go to her assistance, and trying desperately to smother the giggles that bubbled up inside us, she solved the problem by yelling at us to come and help her. To us her language was anything but lady-like. As we drew nearer, to our joy the chair miraculously fell away and the lady stood upright, shaking with laughter. Looking at us she said, 'Oh go on, let it rip; have a jolly good guffaw.'

We hardly knew what that strange word meant but soon we were all doing just that. Between us we managed to get the chair fixed up again.

'Well, kids, what do you want?', she asked when our giggles had stopped. 'You see', she added, 'I am Cross by name but not by nature, aren't I?' Her name was Mrs Cross and the house was called Crossways.

Presently a maid appeared and Mrs Cross told her to

'Bring something for these kids to eat'. Although we did not like being referred to as the off-spring of nanny goats, it did not take us long to accept the thick slices of fruit cake and glasses of cool lemonade. Her husband appeared and asked me, 'If you would like some more cake, which would you choose - quality or quantity?'

Then he drew a plate of cakes towards us. Demurely I said, 'I had better have quantity, then we can share it with the other girls; but I guess quality would be best for one or two.' Both Mr and Mrs Cross seemed to find this hilarious. Mr Cross let out a real bellow of gusty laughter and Mrs Cross produced another hearty guffaw. Eventually, after being laden with slabs of cake 'for the other kiddies', we suddenly realised that we had been there a long time; we turned and walked down the drive with many 'thank yous' echoing behind us. As we went we realised that one of us was still holding the card we had come to deliver.

Among the houses I liked visiting was one situated at the end of a lane called The Cut, leading from one main road to another. Two girls were sent there each week during the First World War carrying deep straw fish-baskets, ostensibly to collect the scraps for the rabbits we kept. At the house we called on the cook-housekeeper who was a friend of matron. She would fill our baskets with vegetable peelings, outer lettuce leaves, apple peelings, pea pods and other so-called waste.

While exploring the contents of these baskets one day, we discovered that some of the pea-pods were not empty shucks; sweet young carrots lay among the peelings at the bottom of the bags. Some of these extras did not reach their proper destination. It was quite a while before our guilty secret was revealed, and two other girls were given the job.

During the soft fruit season we were invited to go to this house and pick the blackcurrants, raspberries, redcurrants and a few whitecurrants. The bushes were in an enclosed part of the garden, covered in to prevent the birds from helping themselves. Once we had picked the amount required by the housekeeper for bottling and jam-making, we could have some for ourselves as a reward. Two or three kinds of gooseberry grew there too and I particularly like the fat green-gold ones: I believe they were called Golden Drops. Some were dark-red and more bristly and not so juicy but each had their special use and flavour. We enjoyed this task.

The cheeriness and good nature of the housekeeper were not the only reasons I liked going to this house. The Cut seemed to me a little paradise: at all seasons there were flowers along the length of it; in winter we found a few hazel catkins with strange buds which had red thread-like bits showing. Later in the year, they were soft to the touch. As they ripened the nut-shell became hard. I wonder how many people have tasted the delicious milky-warm hazel nut straight from the bough.

Among the first flowers were the bright gold celandines, cheery and glowing; and daisies could be relied on any time. I have a special affection for these often despised and ill-treated flowers - they teach us a lesson in persistence: no matter how badly they are treated they go on growing. At school we were told that they represented the British Empire: many small parts each having its own special place to make a complete flower - and so our colony made up our Empire.

How strange that the dull dusty purple deadnettle acquired the name of Archangel. Queen Anne's lace - frothy and fragrant - adorned the sides; dog-violets, daisies, dandelions, forget-me-nots, bird's eye, speedwell and all manner of wild flowers grew in the lane.

Another lady we visited lived in a house with a long, dark drive which was mossy underfoot; sombre conifers lined each side. Quite often we would see a squirrel or two, and have cones dropped on our heads while the culprit in the tree above stayed hidden. A rather forbidding notice a little way inside the drive stated: 'Private. Trespassers will be prosecuted'; some girls would read that last word as 'persecuted'. We were glad to see the house at the end of the drive and would not have liked to walk along the drive after dark. A maid would open the door when we rang the bell and we were shown into an inner room and kindly received by the lady of the house who was deaf and used an ear-trumpet. She painted pictures of Jesus as a child and used the name Irlam Briggs. Some of the pupils of St. Peter's school were used as models; she did not use any one boy for the Christ-child, but selected the best feature from different boys, saying that only the best would show the real Jesus.

Many years later a curious coincidence occurred in connection with these pictures. My own two children attended a small school and church in a Wiltshire village. I used to do needlework for the Vicar's wife; discussing the subject of prizes for Sunday-school children, I put forward the idea that perhaps a small framed picture would be a change from the usual books. The idea was adopted and both my children received prints of pictures by Irlam Briggs! I could identify some of the girls who had been at the school which I attended.

On rare occasions a lady would invite a few of us to tea; we talked about our interests and possible ambitions for the future. We had lovely thin bread and butter, jam and cake, and the cups, saucers and plates were of very dainty china so that we were almost afraid to use them. The was all part of the treat.

At one house we were shown into a conservatory, and told to put earphones on our heads, two girls at a time. Presently we heard faint, rather scratchy music coming, we were told, from the Winter Gardens in Bournemouth. It seemed quite uncanny to us.

Another time we went to tea with a lady who had a gramophone with a big blue horn that played music. I was very small then and kept looking to see where the voice of the singer was coming from. The song was 'Robin, robin, redbreast, oh, robin dear; robin sings so sweetly at the falling of the year'.

The girls from St. Faiths

'Memory is a rag-bag...'

Memory can be like so many different things. At the moment memory seems like a rag-bag; a rag-bag was very much part of our lives then: into a large bag, itself made from oddments, went scraps of material kept in case they 'came in handy'. Now, I dip into my rag-bag of memory and wonder which snippet I will draw out; one thought or word may set off a stream of happenings not necessarily in chronological order. During the night, when all is quiet, is a good time to dip into my rag-bag of memory and I keep a pad of paper to jot down ideas as they come.

Now, I have drawn an incident from the rag-bag about the time two girls tried to run away from St. Faiths. Somehow they had contrived to get kept in after lessons at school, which was a punishment for small misbehaviour. When the rest of us assembled to walk home in our crocodile they could not be found. We discovered later they had been hiding in the lavatories. We waited a while and then decided to go on, thinking of possible reasons for their absence: maybe they were having a telling-off from the head-mistress, or perhaps one girl had been unwell and the other had taken her home earlier. So off we went.

There was no sign of them at home and there was much whispered surmising about their whereabouts from the groups of girls in the schoolroom. Teatime came and still they had not turned up. Things began to look serious; the police were informed as the girls had to be found before dark. All enquiries and searching was done personally - there were no telephones at St. Faiths. Some of the older girls went out in pairs to look in nearby places. Matron stayed at the Home in case they turned up. Most of us were not old enough to realise the seriousness of the situation. We looked on it as a kind of adventure bringing a bit of excitement in our lives.

After quite a while, the two runaways were brought back. They had been found hiding in some heather, at a spot about a mile and a half away, called 'The Bunny', near the railway line between Parkstone and Poole Stations. They had set out to find the way to Weymouth where one of them had a father living, by following the railway lines.

So much for youthful dreams. When they were brought in

they were tired, cold and hungry but had to be content with dry bread and water for a day or two. I think they were given a hot drink - I cannot think that Miss Langley would have sent them to bed on dry bread and cold water. The whole affair was hushed up and forgotten though we girls made the most of it for a while among ourselves.

Many incidents and personalities from our girlhood days have been forgotten but one character remains fairly clear in my remembrance. This gentleman was one of the benefactors we included in our nightly prayers. We used to see him sometimes on our way to and from school. He looked very old and was always alone when we saw him; in some vague way we felt sorry for him. He always wore a top hat with a wide crepe band with two ends hanging over the brim at the back. We were told that his name was Doctor Dobell, with the letters D.D. after it. This puzzled us as we had no idea what these letters signified. When we heard that they stood for Doctor of Divinity we felt a sense of awe. Vaguely, I thought he had some connection with St. John, the Divine to whom the Book of Revelation is credited.

Doctor Dobell had a gentle, kindly face, all wrinkled; he could smile with his eyes. Although we were a tiny bit 'afeared' of him, we had a mild affection for the old gentleman. Every year in March, each child received a gift of a bright new shilling which were given in memory of his wife.

When we saw him we would call across to him if he was on the other side of the road; we were not supposed to break ranks. However, we knew that he would come over and speak to us. He always carried nuts in one coat pocket and sweets in the other and he would ask each one of us to choose which we would like. Crafty little beggars, we must have been: some girls would choose a nut and say that it was bad - then they would get a sweet as well. I am sure he was aware of our trick even though we thought he seemed absent minded.

Eventually one February, news came that he had died. He had requested that some of the girls from St. Faiths should attend his funeral. A glass-walled carriage was ordered to take us to the church and cemetery . It was a cold, drizzly day. The black horses had glossy coats and black plumes which moved rhythmically up and down as they walked. The sad-faced coachman, Mr Swain, had a truly gloomy Dickensian countenance. He had a black bow on his whip and crepe round his hat. We each wore a wide black ribbon armband on our coat sleeves. Although we felt it was a sad and solemn occasion, we could not help feeling a thrill riding in a carriage and pair.

After the church ceremony, we were driven to the cemetery

which was quite a distance away and approached by a long avenue of trees. We shivered, partly with cold and partly with a sense of fear as we saw the deep hole into which the coffin was lowered. It was the first funeral we had ever attended. The greyness of the day and the plop of the clod of earth - not in the least like 'dust to dust' - seemed to set a seal on a sad and solemn day.

The worthy gentleman was interred in the same grave as his wife and there were many beautiful floral tributes which we were allowed to look at afterwards. I read the words engraved on the granite curb which had been set on its side near the grave. For a very long time they did not make sense to me. The text was in black letters: 'Except the Lord build the house, their labour is but vain that build it.'

On the return journey we were not allowed to ride in the carriage. We were told that it would be rather too much like a treat, and that respect must be shown for the one who had passed away. Although we did not have to walk in pairs, we had to be sober and quiet. The walk was about a mile and a half and we were cold with frozen hands and feet, yet no one grumbled; we felt a genuine sense of loss for someone we had known for a long time. Some time later each child had a gift of five shillings.

In those days funerals always were more solemn and elaborate, slow and dignified. The deceased was not hurried away: due ceremony had to be observed, even before the day of the funeral. It was customary for all blinds or curtains facing the house in the road where the person had lived and died to be drawn across while the cortege passed by; men would always doff their hats and women stand with bowed heads when outdoors. On the day of death, the church bell would ring: one stroke for a man, two for a woman and three for a child. Afer a minute of silence the bell would toll as many strokes as the age of the deceased.

Another person very much involved in our lives was a lady who lived in Mount Road. She and her sisters were daughters of the Sheriff of Poole. Miss Elspie, as we called her, came voluntarily once or twice a week to teach us singing and dancing. How our ancient piano must have frayed her nerves, to say nothing of the efforts of girls like myself who simply cannot sing - no amount of teaching can make nightingales out of starlings. Most of the girls enjoyed these lessons although some preferred the dancing; but I was too fat and not built for this activity either.

Miss Elspie was gentle, kind and forbearing, and would provide any girl who had throat trouble or other minor ailments, with lozenges and cough medicine. One day the piano sounded even worse than usual and seemed to have something wrong inside: the notes were flat and muffled. On opening the top and peering into the works, Miss Elspie found several bright pink capsules stuffed down among the wires. The shame of that discovery: these were pills she had generously given to the girls who suffered from chilblains. Her forbearance must have been sorely tested but I do not remember her reaction. I wonder she did not abandon us from that moment but I do not think that she even 'let on' to Miss Langley about this ingratitude.

I remember another episode concerning Miss Elspie. During one summer a series of tableux depicting stories from the Bible, were held in the garden of St. Peter's Vicarage. Canon R. E. Adderly was the vicar at that time. About ten or twelve girls were chosen to form a choir and sing hymns appropriate to each picture represented: girls and boys from St. Peter's School were the figures in the Tableaux. Those of us who were not in the choir went along to rehearsals to make up an audience.

One evening, Miss Elspie happened to be passing the garden and heard children's voices and thought how good the choir sounded. She went in to see who was singing with the idea of congratulating them. To her astonishment it was 'her' girls from St. Faiths. Somehow the powers-that-be had slipped up and Miss Elspie had not been consulted to ask if we might appear and sing in public.

One of Miss Elspie's sisters was involved with the suffragette movement, and like many others, went to prison for a spell in her effort to get Votes for Women. We secretly thought it rather exciting and courageous.

They had an old English sheepdog called Bill, who was a favourite with some of us. He would come bounding and lolloping to greet us, unaware that his very size made him rather fearsome to the little ones, although he was really very gentle and good-tempered.

Some time during my girlhood the powers-that-be suggested forming a Girl Guide Troop. Miss Elspie became our Captain and two Patrols were formed. I was one of the eldest girls and became a leader of the Thrush Patrol. Louie was leader of the Robins. As we were not enough to form a proper Company we were merged with the 1st Parkstones and became the 3rd Parkstones.

Generally speaking, our standards were modest in some subjects. Probably we had certain limitations in the higher standards of education: classical music, art, sports - such as tennis, hockey, cricket. The girls in the 1st Parkstone Troop mostly attended Sandecotes School - described as being for the 'daughters of gentlefolk': to us they seemed rich and strange. Many of the subjects they discussed were above our heads. We felt that some of them thought of us as little 'ninnys'. However, most of them were kind to us and helped our efforts in unfamiliar subjects.

We came into our own when we tried for the Domestic Science badge: we were better adapted to the practical issues of - what we called - housework; menial tasks such as washing, ironing, making a bed properly, turning out a room to give it a good clean, polishing cutlery were almost unknown to the young ladies of the gentry, who often had servants.

Guiding brought another lady into our lives, Miss Gracie Haskitt-Smith, our Lieutenant. I and another girl from the Home remained her friends until Miss Gracie's death in 1963.

Guiding took up a good deal of our time and energy. We had to find ways and means of getting the money to pay for our uniforms and make our own dresses. We attended various functions which most of us enjoyed.

On one occasion we formed part of the Guard of Honour when the Duke of York, later to become King George VI, came to open a Doctor Barnardo's Nautical School. It was a very hot day, and several 1st Parkstone Guides fainted. Our Lieutenant was busy attending to them and I, not having much gump, did not give the word of dismissal after the ceremony. There we stood, stiffly to attention, till she returned.

Another time we went to a County Rally at Upton House, the home of Miss LLewellyn, the County Commissioner. To our surprise we received a commendation for smartness from Miss Baden-Powell who was the visiting V.I.P. I remember her telling us that as she was wearing a gold boomerang brooch which had recently been presented to her by Girl Guides in Australia and made of Australian gold, she was breaking one of the Guide rules: the only badge allowed to be worn while in Girl Guide uniform was the Trefoil Leaf Badge.

As well as joining the Girl Guides we also belonged to the Band of Hope, a Temperance Society. We met every Saturday afternoon in a rather dingy hall in Lower Parkstone. We did needlework and knitting for their sale of work. Occasionally we gave concerts to which the public were invited and sang songs mostly about the evils of strong drink and performed short plays on the same theme.

Fleeting fragments stir in my memory and at odd moments flash through my mind: I will set them down quickly before they escape forever. These oddments clamour to be included but are not in chronological order.

While at school a dreadful disaster shook the whole nation. One day in April, 1912 the wonderful, so-called 'unsinkable' ship, Titanic, sunk: nearly everyone on board perished.

The next day when all classes were assembled after prayers and the register had been called, the headmistress announced the tragedy; then we sung the hymn, 'For those in peril on the sea'. Although I was only nine years old I thought it was silly to ask God to save them when so many lives had been lost. At least two pupils - a brother and sister - lost their father in this tragedy. We were all very subdued.

A secret childish ambition was roused whenever I saw the firechief run down Mount Road to join the other firemen at the main road whenever there was a fire. In my mind's eye I can see him in dark-blue uniform, fastening the buckle on his belt as he ran. His silver helmet swung by its strap on his arm. How I longed to wear that lovely shiny helmet for a moment. We knew he was the chief because the other men had brass helmets. I would have been more than happy to have had a word spoken to me or a smile from my hero, but he had more important things to do than notice a little girl with an unspoken ambition.

In contrast to visions of myself donning a silver helmet, is the memory of the plaits we put on our heads when we played indoors or in the woods. These adornments were made of rag cut into strips and plaited and stitched on to a head band: we called them 'toscarts'. We let them fall in front of each side of our heads, then tossed them over our shoulders trying to imitate the feminine gesture of girls with plaits of their own hair. With an assortment of dressing-up clothes we felt quite grand.

A happening comes to mind that could have ended in disaster, but fortunately did not. One day, during playtime, a bull, being driven to the nearby abattoir, broke loose and headed for the playground. Never have girls gone into school so quickly: screaming and pushing, some became stuck in the narrow lobby doorway. Rather than feeling fear, I was curious to see what the bull would do, but, being small, I was crushed in the tight pack and some girls were in greater danger of being injured by each other than by the bull which was quickly captured. Of course, once safely inside we were brought to order by the teacher but our concentration was somewhat lacking during afternoon lessons.

At school the girls had to use the boys' playground for drill as there was not enough room in the girls' playground when two classes joined together for these lessons. While marching round and round some girls would drop out of line, ostensibly to fasten a shoelace, but it was a sly dodge to attract the attention of any passing boy. Eventually teacher found a solution: all girls had to spend most of the time in learning to tie shoelaces in a bow that would not come undone unless pulled - it was known as a Victoria Bow.

One of the highlights of our summer holidays from school was going to 'toss the hay'. We went to a field belonging to a lady who lived near Sandbanks. She arranged for us to go to a hayfield in the horse-brake. There we had a wonderful time playing. This was a recognised method of helping to dry the hay, and though we did not actually stack it into stooks, we piled it into rather untidy heaps. When we had finished our work, a long table was set up out of doors, spread with all sorts of interesting food; we were told to tuck in and you may be sure we did.

One day, when it was time to go home, two girls were found to be missing. A search was made in the hayfield; then someone spotted a pair of legs underneath the cloth on the trestle table: there were the two culprits busily engaged in licking all the sugar off the pretty biscuits and stuffing other goodies inside their garments for later consumption. One of the naughty girls was - can you guess? - me! Probably Louie was the other one. The lady would not allow the others to scold us; instead she gave the other girls some more biscuits to take back. You can be sure we were not allowed to forget our greedy behaviour by the other girls.

Another vivid memory is of the first time that I heard bird-song. I had been out to the lav at the back of the house. On coming out I heard a wonderful sound: I stood absolutely transported, uplifted with a strange wonderful inward joy at the beauty of the sound. At first I could not see where it was coming from but after a while traced it to the branches of a sycamore tree near the back gate. I was not supposed to be there but I did not care - I had to find out what was making such a thrilling sound. By standing still and keeping quiet, I looked up into the tree and among the canopy of leaves was a black bird with a bright yellow beak; I could see its throat vibrating and listened, wrapped in a magic world of my own. That a black bird could pour out such music was a miracle to me. That was the first time I realised that bird could sing. It lasted only a few minutes but it has given me a lifetime's memory. Another day I saw a huge bird in a treetop, and said I had seen an eagle; but it was only a rook or crow, magnified by a childish imagination.

More unconnected items crowd my mind for recognition. One concerns fragmented mind pictures and impressions at the time of the Coronation of King George V and Queen Mary. Of course, we did not attend directly any of the jubilations or ceremonies; we only heard faint echoes and had an extra holiday from school. All school children in the Borough of Poole were presented with a Coronation mug with a design in raised figures of the new King and Queen on it, and a small tin box of chocolates. There were twenty-four tiny cream-filled chocolates in a box about the size of the tip of one's little finger and a picture of royalty on the lid. I still have the tin - the only discernable thing is the faint name of the chocolate makers on the bottom of it.

Although we could not join in the celebrations, we could see the glow of the huge bonfire on the top of Constitution Hill - one of many lit all over the country. Warm ashes lay about in a blackened circle for several days after. Charabancs would bring people to see the lovely view all across Poole Harbour, someone would discover the remains of the fire and toss out pennies and we would try and pick them up still rather hot. How we ever managed to go there and behave in such an undignified way, scrambling in black ashes for coins, I have forgotten. Neither do I know how we accounted for a sudden extra flow of cash or how we spent it. Children can be quite resourceful when necessary.

One day I was out at the back having been to 'spend a penny' when I heard a strange noise, like nothing I had ever heard before. It was rather frightening but I crept to the back gate and peeped along the main road. I had seen this odd creature in picture books - a man dressed in an odd-looking garment was walking by the side of an elephant. I hurried back to tell the other girls who all crept to another spy-hole near the end of the black corrugated fence, out of sight of authority, but alas, the procession had passed out of sight: we dared not go out into the main road to get a better view. To this day I doubt if some of the girls believed my yarn. After all I did invent stories when we were in bed and not supposed to talk.

One day we were allowed to go outside and see the strange sight of the Town Crier as he came along ringing his heavy bell and roaring out any important news. He looked to us a quaint historical figure, dressed in a long coat with a big cape-collar and brass buttons, and a Tricorn hat. His message often foretold the news that all water supplies would be cut off for a time. He would stand for a few moments bellowing that householders should prepare baths and pails of water to use until normal supplies were available again.

Another memory of those days was the water cart drawn by a big heavy carthorse, with sprinklers shooting out jets of water on either side, to lay the dust in very dry weather: not many roads had tarmac surfaces then. It was quite a fascinating sight, especially if the sun caught the trickle in a sunbeam and made a tiny rainbow; it dissolved almost immediately but was delicate and lovely for an instant of time.

One morning we had a nasty fright. It happened as Miss Langley was saying the last of the short morning prayers as we knelt around the schoolroom facing her. She had just started to say 'The grace of our...' but never finished the prayer: she collapsed right there onto the floor. For a second everyone was stunned. We did not like to open our eyes which were closed for praying - but some of us peeped a bit. What we saw shocked us although it was only for an instant: Miss Langley lay on the floor all crumpled up. Matron and Dorothy went quickly to help her up. One of the older girls went for Nellie who came at once and between them Miss Langley was gently carried away. We were completely shattered. It had never dawned on any of us that such a thing could happen to our superintendant. We had an awful vision of illness and death.

Discipline and order were restored and off we went to school as usual. I am sure none of us were very attentive that day; you can imagine what our topic of conversation was about.

By the time we arrived back for dinner the doctor had been and we were told that Miss Langley must have complete rest. She was ill for some time and we really prayed earnestly for her recovery. We could not imagine what our lives would be like without her altogether. We all had a deep respect for her mingled with real affection. However, there were so many girls, love could not be freely shown: no one girl could be singled out for special affection. It was unusual for anyone to kiss away a hurt or cuddle a sad child.

After about a month, some of the older girls were allowed to go in and see her for a few moments, usually in the evening. Eventually she recovered completely.

Another significant happening was the arrival of a particularly virulent influenza. St. Faiths, like other Homes all over the country, had its share of victims. It attacked young and old; even matron, who was seldom ill, was affected. It was a very hard time as those who could have helped with daily work were stricken down and it was impossible to keep any sort of normal routine. We were put in touch with a group of ladies called the V.A.D.s (Voluntary Aid Detachment) who had done wonders during the War. They came to our rescue very quickly; two ladies whose names were the Misses Walters arrived at an early hour and did jobs which I am sure they were not really brought up to do, being well-to-do and having servants of their own. They did everything from taking temperatures to washing and dressing the tinies and bringing hot meals to those who could eat them. To patients who were making good progress they would smile and say, 'Capital, capital', so quite naturally they were called the Capital sisters. I do not know how we could have managed without them. When we had all recovered they invited us over to their house to tea. Later, they were instrumental in getting me my first place in service as a between-maid.

Below are some curious words and sayings:

* Snuggle-tooth - this indicated a gap in one's mouth where a tooth had been; perhaps the original word was 'snaggle-tooth'.
* Sugar-baby - this word was used for girls who did not like going out in the rain.
* Swank-pot - a name given to a girl who showed off.
* Loppy-legs - this was chanted at someone whose plain-hemmed drawers showed below their dress.
* Saturday night's reaches / Cat's teeth - two ways of describing stitches which were not as neat and small as they should be.
* Cowardy cowardy custard, eat your mother's mustard:
  I hope it chokes you.

This was chanted to someone who would not take up a challenge or dare.
* Tell-tom-tit you want your tonque slit,
  and every puppy dog will have a bit.

We chanted this at girls who told tales or sneaked.
* If someone was in a bad mood, she was told she had a 'black monkey on her back' and was bidden to get rid of it.
* A superstition - on Fridays nails should not be trimmed, hair cut or mattresses turned.

Leisure

Although discipline was strict we always had some liberty. We had regular periods of play: we would skip, bowl our hoops, or invent games to suit the mood of the moment. We had a scooter but the craze did not last long as scuffing one foot to keep balance wore out one shoe faster that the other. We were not allowed to play ball games or make much noise in the quiet road.

I loved it best when we could play in the pinewoods at the side of the house. This was a favourite place of mine. We were never to go out of sight of the house; there were always the watchful eyes of the older girls to see that we did not get into mischief. Pine cones can be quite a formidable weapon when thrown in a fit of temper, or sudden burst of petulance.

We created circular and square houses with walls made from pine needles. It took skill and patience to make the walls stand higher than a few inches. If some girls did manage a height of a foot or more, Authority bade them be pulled down to less than a foot. (Authority did not have to give reasons - only made decisions.) Inside the houses we held dolls' tea-parties, told stories, read aloud or sung together - although this was not encouraged in case a neighbour might complain. These houses gave us a feeling of belonging to our particular group of friends; no girl could visit another house without an invitation.

We used to gather bright yellow pollen to make into custard for dolls' tea-parties. Being a little taller than Louie I tried to get some water from the butt at the side of the greenhouse, to mix with the pollen. Unfortunately there was only a small amount of water at the bottom; in reaching down for it I overbalanced and my head became stuck, firmly wedged underneath the pipe which took water from the guttering into the rainwater butt. I suppose my yells were too muffled for anyone to hear because it seemed ages before someone discovered a pair of sturdy legs frantically waving in an attempt to get free. My plump body was wedged in a very undignified attitude and my head was just clear of the filthy water.

None of the girls could release me and Authority had to be summoned quickly. I was almost suffocating and the stench from the slimy water was making me feel sick. Dorothy came to the rescue and managed to extricate me, nearly twisting my head off - or so it seemed to me - in her frantic efforts to haul me out. You can be sure that the scent emanating from me was not that of sweet violets. It was unheard of for any girl to have a bath in the daytime but I was soon soaking in lovely hot water with some kind of disinfectant; even the smell of carbolic soap was more pleasant to inhale than rain-water slime. We were not supposed to obtain water in this way, but I escaped with a good telling off for being disobedient - they probably thought I had been punished enough.

When playing in the woods we had to be careful about ants because they could, and did, sting. In the building of our pine houses we would sometimes demolish laboriously constructed ant colonies; then we would cluster round and watch the ceaseless activity, and marvel at the speed at which a new site was made ready to receive the disturbed grubs. This process was a never-ending source of wonder to us.

The older girls had the job of collecting firewood and fircones - quite a pleasant task and worth ½d for six basketsful. This could be an enjoyable task; I loved the tingling scent but the sticky turpentine that oozed out was hard to clean off our fingers. Many a pinafore was used inside out in efforts to wipe the stickiness away or we would be given a 'bad mark' - a phrase which often cropped up in our lives.

A job which was less favoured was gathering manure - a bonus left by tradesmen's horses which used the cul-de-sac. A large rusty fish-kettle, discarded from its original purpose, had to be filled six times for the price of one penny. Two girls had to take turns each day, weather permitting, for this delectable job; they had old fire shovels and a flat piece of wood to push the spoils on the shovel. We did not wear gloves or mittens on our hands unless it was very cold.

One day I made an uncomplimentary remark to one of the 'collectors' - an older girl than myself. She appeared at first to take no notice but a moment later the contents of the pot were tipped over my head from behind and the pot rammed down. Luckily it did not fit too tightly, but the problem was how to clean up without being discovered by the 'powers that be': Authority must not be let into our dirty secret! I have a vague recollection that another girl rinsed my hair with rain-water from the butt and dried it with her pinny. No wonder I developed a mop of thick unruly, wiry hair in later years.

We became familiar with creepy-crawlies: some girls disliked spiders, others disliked earwigs or centipedes, but I think most of us liked the bright-red chubby ladybirds. In those days I had never seen the larval stage of this insect, and even now find that few people connect the rather queer looking blue-and yellow grub with its parent ladybird. We did not care much for the hairy caterpillars, or the yellow-and-black striped ones devouring ragwort at a fantastic rate. I think we, horrid creatures, would quite gaily collect worms and rush to feed the wriggling creatures to the hens and chicks which Nellie looked after. Probably the sight of the yellow fluffy chicks was sufficient reward for handling the squirming worms. I wonder how we managed to pass the kitchen window without the eye of Authority spotting us - maybe even that was blind at times.

I suppose I always had an interest in Natural History, though I kept it secret for many years, especially when, in my teens, I was teased unmercifully by girls who found an entry in my diary which read, 'Saw some swifts flying low.' Botany appealed to me: I still have some laboriously pressed flowers in blotting paper stuck inside exercise books and labelled with names, sometimes with an appropriate verse written on the opposite page.

I realise, now, how fortunate we were to have Miss Langley to guide us into paths of knowledge. We were encouraged to study every aspect of nature, except, strangely enough, we learned nothing of the mating and birth of animals around us. We saw lambs and calves in the fields around but had no idea how they came into being, we knew only that birds laid eggs which hatched into chicks.

Someone gave us two guinea pigs called Bright Eyes and Sobersides. A small hutch was made which they did not like and they rubbed their noses sore on the wire netting: they had probably been used to a larger run on a lawn. One day it would seem that the door was not too securely fastened: exit Bright Eyes and Sobersides.

Most of us enjoyed tending our small gardens which made splashes of colour ana each one varied according to individual fancy. One year I had a passion for pansies and my plot was full of little pansy faces 'growing in the garden fair', urged on to prodigious size by frequent applications of a product bought in a green-and-gold tin from a shop near St. Peter's Church. It was called 'Canary guano'. For a long time we thought it was provided by canary birds and wondered how such small birds could exist in large enough flocks to supply this bonus for our plants. Later, we learnt that it was gathered from the free-will offerings of much larger birds dwelling in and around the Canary Islands. The smell when we first opened the tin was almost like being gassed but its strength waned as it was frequently exposed to the air; it worked wonders for our little plots and was more convenient to use that the horse manure we could get free which attracted horrible maggots and flies.

On summer evenings, from 6.30 until 7.30, the middle girls had a sewing hour in the garden. By then the older girls had indoor jobs and had to listen for any sound from the little ones. We enjoyed those sewing meetings, except on Mondays which was the night for darning socks and stockings; these had been washed on Saturday and, after being dried and aired, were sorted and put in a pile from which we each drew out a quota to be darned. Miss Langley, who read a story to us while we worked, examined every one: her long fingers soon found any weak spot which became a hole as she probed and returned it to the mender. We were taught to do proper darning by an older girl: as the wool would be new but not the garment, we were shown how to leave loops of the wool at each end of a darn to allow for shrinkage in the wash. We were not allowed to use a 'mushroom' - a small wooden object with a short handle - which was put inside the sock to make it easier to tackle large holes. Sometimes I used my fist or occasionally a small tin but it seemed like cheating.

Memory stirs and prods during a sleepless hour and I am reminded that I have not mentioned the summer outings we had. If I do not record them they will be lost.

Outings to Sandbanks during the school summer holidays were one of the highlights of our childhood days. When the great day came how eagerly we would press our faces close to the window to try and be the first to see the brake come up the road, drawn by two horses. How closely we studied the weather: if it was inclined to rain we earnestly prayed for the sun to shine. In retrospect, it usually did and I cannot recall any real disappointments due to wet days.

St. Faiths owned, or possibly rented, a fairly large hut set among the sand-dunes at Sandbanks. It was a quiet place with few houses and only small hotels. The journey there was about five miles; there was not enough room for all the girls to ride in the brake, even if some sat on the floor instead of on the thinly padded seats along the sides. It always smelt of manure and straw which was spread about on the floor of the brake.

The arrangement was for some of the older girls to walk

halfway; they would wait by the Beehive Hotel for the brake to arrive; this was considered to be a fair distance for either walkers or riders to make the change-over. I used to try and ride the first part of the journey because the second part seemed much more interesting to walk.

One particular attraction was the sight of hundreds of gulls: swooping, wheeling, swerving and screaming above and around the Corporation rubbish dump. This is now a pleasant grassed-over site with swings and other joys for children and seats for all who can spare time to watch the activities going on in this backwater of Poole Harbour.

Another lovely view-point is at the top of Evening Hill: nowadays, there are many yachts with sails of all colours lying at anchor or moving in and out on their various businesses. Brownsea Island and smaller isles lie dotted about the harbour. It is a picture I never tire of seeing and rivals anywhere I have seen on my travels - especially on a fine summer day.

We used to like walking along the top of the curved wall between the road and the shore. As children we were seldom out late enough to see the street lamp lit: a man with a long pole, riding a bicycle, would stop at each one and pull a chain to start the gas-mantle glowing.

Eventually we arrived at the hut and almost fell out of the brake; the walkers would take a short-cut across the dunes, each girl crying to be first. Exciting parcels and packets were brought out from the brake; two Beatrice oil stoves were filled, wiped clean and lit ready for the big iron kettles to be put on. They took a long time to boil: water had to be fetched in galvanised buckets from the coast guards hut a short distance away. Water cost ½d a bucket - we were very careful not to spill any as we made our way over the dry, shifting sand and between the hummocks. It was all too exciting for us to really notice the weight of the buckets we carried.

Innocent by today's standards we may have been; but somehow we never felt at ease with the man at the hut: instinct warned us in a subtle way that we should never be alone with him. We would never accept his smiling invitation to go in and see his watercolour pictures around the walls, interesting though they appeared by the glimpse we had from outside. This sensitivity was too vague to be mentioned to the grown-ups.

It did not take long to fill the big black kettles which were then placed very carefully on the smoky oil stoves. Plates and enamel mugs were brought out from a cupboard in the hut. Bread and marge and cold meat sandwiches, bottles of milk and lemonade were put out of the sun; the little ones could hardly wait to shed shoes and socks and race down to the beach. However much sand the sandwiches acquired they seemed to taste extra good, as did the strong, dark tea. Two shallow blue enamel baking tins held rice pudding, already cooked and so stiff it was cut into chunks and eaten like cake. Sometimes, to our joy, we had lumps of heavy, yummy bread pudding, sticky and sweet, although the crispy crust had become a bit too tough and rubbery. It clung to our teeth but was wholly enjoyable.

No wonder we were not allowed to bathe at least an hour after such a meal. If we promised not to go out too far we could paddle. Rules were a bit relaxed, up to a point. Quickly plimsols were discarded, socks stuffed inside before putting them, tied in pairs, underneath the hut which had a fair space for such uses. Dresses and petticoats were hastily tucked into bloomers - garments not usually seen or mentioned - often not verv securely. Middle girls each grabbed her own little charge and off they would scamper in haste to reach the enticing sea before anyone else.

Oh, the delicious feel of the first gentle wavelets kissing our toes and of sand being drawn like silk from underneath our feet, leaving dents in the spot where we had been standing. This was one of the simplest and most enjoyable of childhood's pleasure; also the taste of salt on our lips, the sparkle of the golden sun on the water and on our limbs, the blue of the sky, white clouds reflected as different colours in the sea water, rippling waves, patterns on the wet sand, gulls wheeling overhead, perhaps even a white-sailed yacht - all combining to create an unforgettable picture. Although we were too busy enjoying ourselves to take it in at the time, I suppose we stored it in our subconscious; I know that I could conjure it all up again in bed during the quiet darkness of another night when I was less tired from the day's activities.

After a suitable interval while the grown-ups rested or as they would say, had 'forty winks', we were told we could get ready for bathing; the tinies were not included in this ritual. How I wish I had kept some of the old snapshots. I shall never know how the elders were not dragged down by the sheer weight of their bathing dresses. They were made of a heavy kind of serge material, frilled at the wrists and ankles, and a bathing cap made of rubber which looked like a pudding cloth, intended to keep the hair dry.

Miss Langley had an inflexible rule that she would dip every girl under the water. She must have had many bruises made by fingers gripping her arm as she dunked each girl under - in our imagination - the huge, threatening waves. Most of us were secretly afraid but we could not escape this ritual, however artful we tried to be. If any one seemed to be getting away, one of the victims who had already been ducked would yell out, 'Cowardy, cowardy custard': it was less of an ordeal to endure the cold water for a few seconds - though it seemed much longer - while the taunting would go on for goodness knows how long.

After the initial baptism we could splash and play for the next ten or fifteen minutes. Oddly enough we were never taught to swim, perhaps none of the adults could do so themselves. I enjoyed floating with outstretched arms and straightened legs on top of the waves with my eyes shut. I never remember matron going for a bathe.

We girls did not wear caps: with our cropped hair it did not matter if it had a dose of sea water. Nevertheless, it left our hair sticky; there were no conveniences of any sort in those days so we could not rinse the sand and salt away. We shivered a bit as we came out all goose-pimply until we were able to dress discreetely in the lee of the hut. For the rest of the day we were gritty with sand, but somehow it was a lovely feeling. For an hour or so we could wander at will along the beach but on no account lose sight of the little ones, or go more than ankle deep into the sea again. Imagine the competition to gather, not the most shells, but the rarest; any girl who found a cowrie, horn or other special shell was almost elected queen of the shore for the rest of the day. (Even now I can not walk along a beach without shell hunting or having a paddle - if there are not many folk about).

As a very special treat, a few of us were taken by the ferry boat across to Shell Bay where the delicate shells were more numerous and there were very few people. The ferry was a small rowboat and I have a suspicion that the ferryman 'forgot' to collect our pennies.

One piece from the Bible (Matthew, chapter 7, verses 24-29) which we had to learn by heart was about the man who built his house on rock foundation which floods and winds could not destroy, and the man who built his house on sand - 'and the rain descended and the floods came and beat upon that house, it fell, and great was the fall of it'. One piece of evidence shown to us there was called 'Simpson's Folly' which was the remains of a house apparently built without firm foundations. All that was left of it was part of a stairway with steps so thick, some tinies needed help to get up them. They were made of concrete embedded with small pebbles and shingle with a pinky-coloured top to each slab.

They led nowhere and probably some were buried in the sand; it gave us a thrill and sense of adventure to clamber about on this ruin.

We were not allowed to roly-poly down the sand dunes or slither down by having one's legs pulled to hasten descent: it was not ladylike behaviour; even so the days at Sandbanks were beacons of brightness in our rather orderly lives.

After tea, there was the job of clearing up and making sure that nothing was left behind. Then perhaps a quick sneaky rush back to the sea for a paddle, before the thrill of the ride home. If the weather turned wet or chilly somehow we all packed into the brake: many would be too sleepy to care how tightly we were squeezed in. It was all part of the day's treat.

If anyone could keep awake there might be a lovely sunset to complete the happy day. This was a sight we were not often out late enough to see and the windows of the Home did not face in the right direction for sunrise or sunset.

At the end of the journey, I have a vague notion that we would give the horses sugar knobs. Their large teeth would put some of us off from performing this kindly deed which I am sure the patient horses richly deserved. I doubt if the sad-faced driver, Mr Swain, even had a glass of ale, but he almost smiled when he left us - perhaps he did not have much in his life to smile at.

Like many other places today, Sandbanks has changed out of all recognition. There are more houses and the hotels are much larger, there is even a tiny church near the end of the road leading to the floating bridge which replaced the ferry rowboat. I believe the first one was purchased from the Isle of Wight some years ago. I still love Sandbanks. If Anniversaries were red letter days, outings to Sandbanks were golden days.

On another occasion we went on a trip to Corfe Castle. All the middle girls went; we congregated in an excited group on Parkstone Station and could hardly wait until our train arrived. Once in the train we were not allowed to be a nuisance. To me it was sufficient to look out of the window and see the countryside as it rushed past; the trees appeared to waltz round and round, and telegraph wires seemed to go up and down. Cows and horses hardly stopped grazing as the train went by, though horses would sometimes run away across the field, tossing their heads as they ran. Cottages had pretty gardens and there seemed a lot of open spaces. We did not fully realise that Dorset is a county of heathlands with acres of golden gorse in spring time, and purple heather for the autumn scene.

Once at Corfe, we had almost perfect freedom, the only limit being that we should keep in groups, no girl straying too far from the others. Being a keen collector of flowers I was perfectly happy to wander about finding specimens for my pressed-flower books. The tiny flowers growing underfoot in the short grass fascinated me and I was eager to learn their names. How good it is to know now that gathering wild flowers is discouraged, and some species are even protected by law. This is all to the good but I do not think that we ravaged the countryside for the few that we wanted. Miss Langley would not have tolerated any form of greed or wanton destruction; moderation in all things was a motto we had to obey.

Corfe Castle stands on a pudding-shaped hillock between the rolling Purbeck Hills; it is one of the most historic ruins in England. It must have possessed a terrible grandeur when it was built and even as a ruin it is imposing, dominating the whole scene. In spite of its grim history, it is saved from being a morbid, forbidding shadow by the gentle rounded slopes of the other hills. Because of its appearance and that of the old grey-stone cottages of the village nestling at the foot of the castle mound, it has become very well known. Many of the cottages had white or yellow stonecrop growing on the roofs and ivy-leaved toadflax and valerian sprouting from the old walls. The greensward was full of flowers and we found graceful quaking grass which we called 'wiggle-woggles', and dainty harebells. Thereby hangs a tale: I spotted some rare white harebells and I gathered as many as I could see. Then I yelled out to the others, 'White harebells!' By then, of course, there were few left and to escape their wrath I tried to run down the hill. I caught my foot in a rabbit hole and rolled down, keeping my eyes shut - just as well that I was plump. As I stopped rolling I heard a snuffling noise and hardly dared open my eyes. I was wedged between a donkey and a gorse bush. I am not sure that I had any precious harebells left or how I managed to get out of my precarious situation. It served me right for being selfish and was a just reward for my mean behaviour.

A further delight on this outing was the lavish spread we were given for our tea; we had it outside in a cottage garden. There were piles of bread and real butter, spread thick, and wads of rich fruit cake and home-made plum jam - still one of my favourites, also biscuits and lemonade. We did full justice to this bounty. I only wish memory would prod me into recalling how it was paid for. I think we each contributed some of our meagre pocket money.

I remember there was a sombre ending to one of our happy outings. As we passed through Poole Station, posters were displayed with big black letters stating 'War Is Declared'. Groups of people were laughing and cheering. I could not understand this; the announcement seemed so grim - surely war was not a thing to rejoice about. We had led sheltered lives and knew nothing of the country's political situation, or the tense state of the nation. We lived in a cocoon, cushioned against the harsher realities of life.

Miss Grainge, Miss Langley and Nellie
Edna, possibly in the centre

War

We experienced little of the War's grimmer aspects. Some of the girls had fathers and brothers in the army or navy. Daisy, who was a little older than me, had only recently discovered her brother and he came to visit her once or twice. Then he joined the Tank Corps, based at Bovington Camp in Dorset. We were very impressed with his smart khaki uniform and black beret; Daisy felt proud to be seen with him. Quite soon after, at the age of nineteen, he was killed. We all felt very sorry for Daisy who was left without any relatives and, in our girlish way, we tried to show her a little extra kindness and to share in her loss.

Those of us with relations living in other towns, especially London, worried about them and prayed for them every night. When the air-raids began I became obsessed with anxiety about my mother and sisters; I knew they were living in London although I had not seen them for a long time. If I did not get a letter just when I expected one, I became withdrawn and anxious, wrapped in my own misery. One day matron took me aside and explained that I was not the only one and that it was useless and selfish to go around looking so unhappy.

At school we were encouraged to write letters to the 'brave boys fighting in the trenches'. We had no real idea of what this phrase meant; it seemed rather silly to me: why should boys be fighting in France, which did not belong to us? I did not know the 'boys' were grown men with families of their own. A few of the older girls did write but no lasting friendships were formed. We also had knitting and sewing classes for making comforts for the troops. I often wondered what really became of our efforts.

One day during a visit to Sandbanks we saw a silvery shape right out on the horizon: it looked rather lovely when the sun shone on it. We were told that it was a German Zeppelin. Another occasion whilst on school holidays, Miss Langley would gather a number of us together and we would stand quietly for a minute and say, 'Give peace in our time, O Lord, for there is none other that fighteth for us, but only you, O God.' It did not seem to do any good. It was all very odd and puzzling - why should God fight for us and if He loved us why did we have wars and kill and wound so many people?

During this time more children arrived at St. Faiths and the number of girls reached twenty-five which was the limit that could be accommodated. Rationing was not so well organised as during the Second World War. We were not familiar with the details of how our food was obtained and did not understand the difficulties of feeding about thirty people. We took it for granted that food would be provided and that our meals would appear as usual.

As time went on and with no end to the War in sight, it became more difficult. We were sent out in twos and threes to visit as many local shops as possible in an attempt to get a half-pound of margarine, or a few potatoes or other goods. These shoppping expeditions provided us with some interest and excitement. One day, Louie and I took a list with us to the shops to buy any available provisions. While we waited to be served at a large grocery shop, a poorly dressed boy came in with a basin. He asked for some glucose: we had no idea what it was. We watched as the assistant took the basin to a barrel and turned on a wooden tap. A stream of white syrup came forth. We stared in wonder and almost forgot what we had come for ourselves. Another day, we had to buy potatoes for the Home. At the shop we were only allowed one pound and to our dismay, there were only two potatoes - a very large one and a smaller one. We were sure the girls in the shop were laughing at our bewilderment - we were almost afraid to take the potatoes home.

It is not surprising that we knew so little about shopping. Normally, groceries were ordered each week and as one lot arrived the man would take the order for the following week and so on - a very practical arrangement. The War changed all that, and we had to forage around and find what we could. Occasionally two girls would go to the same shop, one after the other, hoping to get more that way. Of course, it was obvious where we came from, so often the second girl would get only a quater of marge or come out empty-handed. It must have been a nightmare feeding us all adequately - but I do not remember going without a meal at all.

During the War Years we kept a few rabbits to help with food supplies but I wonder if it was also an attempt to teach us the facts of life. Mrs Doe would disappear now and again and in due course a litter of baby rabbits would appear. Sometimes there were three or four Mrs Does, but only one, or occasionally two, Mr Bucks. If too many girls became over inquisitive and kept going to look at the baby rabbits, we were told that the mother would devour her young. Sacking covers were pulled down in front of the hutches.

Sometimes we did not feel too kindly disposed towards the rabbits. They had insatiable appetites and each time we went for a walk we had to take a rush fish-basket to be filled with dandelion leaves, groundsel and even some soft thistles. If we did try to slip off without one a voice would call, 'Don't forget the rabbit's food.'

As we reached the hutches I'm sure the bunnies could smell the fresh salad we were bringing them: soft noses would twitch and big eyes plead to be given a share of our bounty, which made up for the task of collecting. Hunting for rabbit food gave us a definite reason for going out and not just aimless wandering; I had a quiet botanical hunt for any unusual flowers that grew in verges or hedgerows.

Matron was in charge of the rabbits. She was very conscientious about their health and welfare. She would supervise our attempts to clean out the hutches and make sure that no harmful food found its way among the offerings we gathered. I shall never forget the strong smell of those rabbits and hutches.

Matron was nothing if not ingenious: she had discovered how to treat the skins and make them into small bedside mats. The skins were eventually put on to thick green baize which had a scalloped border all round beyond the fur; they certainly looked most professional and always found a ready sale, sometimes direct to a favoured customer or at the annual sale-of-work.

Preparing the skins was a performance which could not be hurried. The skins had to be very carefully treated; I hope I can rememberd the details correctly. First they were scraped very gently on the inside with the back of a knife. Then they were rubbed with cooking salt which was bought in a block and cost about 2d. This was cut into a heap of loose salt and kept in a big earthenware jar. Sometimes this process had to be repeated because the idea was to rid the skin of any tatters of flesh and veiny bits. When it was really clean it had to dry naturally indoors, away from bright sunlight or drying winds. Usually a day was long enough for this process though it took longer if the weather was damp. The next process was to rub it carefully with alum, which had to be finely powdered as lumps made the drying uneven; this would complete the cleaning and drying. Some skins, of course, were of a better standard than others. A useful product made from poorer quality pelts were fur gloves. The backs and cuffs were made of fur and the hands were knitted or made of chamois leather or other suitable material. They were not as popular as the rugs.

We were filled with youthful enthusiasm when it was proposed we should start an allotment. A field had been acquired and portioned out in long slabs of rough, rank grass, nettles and weeds. Among our male benefactors were some who generously offered their services in making the first dig. Many of them were gentry and unused to such hard labour. Every yard of our territory had to be laboriously dug with spades and forks. Unfortunately, one gentleman lost a gold fountain pen and we all had an unhappy and uncomfortable time being closely questioned by several people. It was never found and in a vague way, we felt inexplicably guilty.

After two seasons of cultivation, back-breaking and frustrating at times, we were encouraged by other helpful allotment-holders to try our luck and enter some vegetables in a local show. To our joy and surprise we were awarded third prize for carrots and beetroot. We could hardly believe that these beautifully coloured and shaped carrots came from the stony, hard, unyeilding earth and were the result of our labours.

One job we heartily disliked was disposing of the little bright yellow wire worms, so prevalent in our first season. We had been advised that the only really safe method was to literally pull them in half or cut them with a spade: it was worse than picking up worms and snails.

One day in a burst of enthusiasm, I stuck a fork right through my big toe, which turned septic. As I was playing the part of Robin Hood in one of our concerts, this was very awkward. How could such a character appear with a bound foot? Jessie, another girl from the Home, who made a much better figure of a man as she was taller, took my place while I had to remain in the background as much as possible. Another effect of this mishap was that I was taken to and from school in a wicker bath chair hired from the church. It seemed important to me to attend because it was the time of the annual scripture examinations. The exams, one-hour each, were held on three separate days: Old Testament, New Testament and Prayer Book. Secretly, I enjoyed the sensation caused when I was wheeled in just before the examination started. I gained first class in all subjects and received a certificate illustrated with a picture of Salisbury Cathedral: St. Peter's Church was in the diocese of Salisbury and the official prize was a set of prayer and hymn books in a little case; I always delighted in the smell and feel of the dark, red crinkly leather.

Strange rumours floated around during those War Years: one

was that spies had put poison in the reservoir at the top of Constitution Hill and that it would make every one in the Borough of Poole sick. No-one could say how the foul deed was done. The only Germans we saw were a party of a dozen prisoners-of-war going up the hill in the charge of a serg-eant. Their coats were very long and they looked shabby and bedraggled. They waved across the road to us as we went down the hill to school. I doubt if any of us had the nerve to wave back.

Memories of the progress of war are vague; but the day War ended is a brighter remembrance. The house at the top of Mount Road was a hospital for Officers. It was a Monday and we were out playing or doing the washing. Then we heard men's voices singing and calling. We were surprised to see many of the officers running down the road, some with arms in slings, some even waving crutches and hobbling along. They shouted out the news as they ran. One or two did a sort of dance and tried to whirl some of the girls around - but the nurses came out and they had to go back.

Those of us who were doing the washing hung our red, white and blue garments on the line. I remember someone looking down into the back-yard from the top of a tram that had stopped; someone called, 'Poor little kids, they have to wear coloured under-clothes'. And that, sadly, is my only clear recollection of the day the Great War ended - November 11th, 1918.

Changes

Eventually, at the age of fourteen, school days came to an end. In a way I was quite sorry to leave. Most of the time I liked school, although I was never any good at games and did not care for playtimes in which girls seemed either to stand around in groups whispering and giggling or else the younger ones rushed round the small playground screaming for no apparent reason.

Although I admit that I was not good at games and only moderately fair at arithmetic, history and geography, my general standard was sufficient for me to be awarded a scholarship for the secondary school. However, there was no possible way that I could take up this opportunity; there were just too many obstacles in the way: setting a precedent, cost of uniform, books and other things and it would have set one girl apart from all the others at St. Faiths. I was partly relieved and a little disappointed, but I had sense enough to accept the situation and stay until time came for me to leave. Some other pupil was more fortunate and took my place.

Once we had left school we had a new daily routine to follow at St. Faiths. Apart from Sunday, each day had its allotted tasks following the general pattern of domestic duties of the period. Inevitably, Monday was Washing Day with the usual frustrating fight to light the copper. This had to be filled bucket by bucket; it had no tap or outlet pipe so our muscles were brought into full play. It was easier for girls who were reasonably tall but I had a job to lift the buckets high enough to empty into the copper, and often became soaked as the water spilt down the front of my clothes, so I was uncomfortable from the start.

Like other coppers I have dealt with since, the fire was temperamental to put it mildly, and subject to the whims and vagaries of wind and weather. Naturally, being the last one to join the work force at that time and the smallest, youngest and least experienced, it fell to me to do the dirtiest, heaviest and most disliked jobs. Wood for kindling had been gathered from the pinewoods and stored in a dry place, but it was often damp and would not light without lots of persuasion - puffing and blowing into the fire which meant lying almost prone on an ash-strewn stone floor.

Joy was intense as the sticks glowed and crackled into life, but was shortlived, as the red glow quickly died unless fed immediately with small knobs of coal and pieces of coke which had to be applied one bit at a time by hand and tenderly placed in just the right spot, or else the first flames would go out. When the fire eventually decided to burn steadily, it could be stoked by the shovel full. This also was an acquired skill.

While the copper was being filled and with the fire going well, clothes were sorted into heaps according to colour and texture. All white articles were first washed by hand in a large heavy zinc bath which stood on strong trestles. This bath had to be filled with hot water from the copper which then had to be replenished in order to boil the whites. Lumps of washing soda were added to soften the water and everything was scrubbed and rubbed using hard soap. This was bought in long yellow bars and cut into squares of handy size and stored on a high shelf to dry in order to make it last longer. Very soiled spots were rubbed with the soap and left to soak while smaller articles were tackled.

After washing and boiling, all the clothes were lifted out of the copper using a wooden copper-stick. This was quite a tricky operation. Sometimes a heavy wodge of clothes would spring into life and splodge over the edge of the copper, showering near-boiling water all over the place.

Next the dripping bunch of clothes had to be lifted into a galvanised bucket, which would be held either by another girl - and seldom in the right position - or by one's own hand while balancing the clothes on the copper-stick with the other hand - an almost impossible feat. It is a marvel to me that no-one was ever scalded badly. Minor splashes were just rubbed with a piece of the yellow soap and, if possible, kept out of the water for a while but were seldom reported to matron.

After the first rinsing in cold water came a second one with a squeeze of the blue-bag in the water: this was intended to make the clothes whiter. There were many different shades of white, from off-white to milky-blue and pale-gray. With the whites safely out of the way on the lines in the back yard, coloureds had their turn and in a way were more interesting. One could never be sure that red or blue garments were fast coloured. Sometimes, in a generous mood, colours would run from one garment to another, giving many others a lovely blushing pink tint or sky-blue shade. The thing that puzzled me was the fact that in the tinted material it was impossible to get the dye out again, and many peculiar shades resulted.

Finally when any woollens had to be done; they were washed in the suds left by the previous coloureds. All the socks and stockings had been washed the previous Saturday, so that they were dry and ready to be mended and paired during Monday evening sewing-time.

Now came the clearing up. All water had to be emptied from the baths into buckets, and in dry weather would be used to water the gardens. Everything, including the copper, baths, buckets, sink, draining board and stone floor had to thoroughly washed and dried. Often horrid scum would have formed, this we slyly scraped off with an old knife, instead of rubbing with home-made scouring powder which took more time and effort.

Monday washday was no picnic, especially in wet or very cold weather, when our hands would get badly chapped and sore. Yet there was a strange satisfaction and sense of achievement in seeing the whites billowing in the breeze and the smell of freshness when we took them all in after a good drying day. Tiredness of limbs was soon forgotten; a sort of inward pride was felt. Now I can appreciate the ease of today's washing fabrics and bright colourful domestic kitchen utensils after our chipped enamel, dingy galvanised and heavy cast-iron pots.

The only articles to be sent out for cleaning were sheets, although half-sized cot sheets were absorbed with other items such as pillow cases and towels. The sheets were laundred by a washerwoman who lived some distance away; they would be called for and brought back in baskets on a hand cart. During one particularly wet period the sheets were not aired to the lady's satisfaction and so a note was enclosed when they were returned to us which read, 'Please her (sic) the sheets.' She lived in a country area called Monkey's Hump, near Heavenly Bottom.

Dinner - however hungry we might be after all our washday efforts - was not one of our favourite meals. It was given the name 'Monday Soup' and was the result of big marrow bones being boiled for hours several days before. There were very little solids added and it was often too greasy to be appetizing. No alternative was forthcoming and our soup bowls were eventually emptied with the help of chunks of rather dry bread. The rice pudding came as a welcome relief, even if it was made with milk and water and was not the creamiest of puds.

In the afternoon, we were allowed to relax or go for a walk or we could do any sewing of our own; or just sit and read. I liked it when we could go into the woods and read a book undisturbed till the others returned from school.

Evenings generally fell into a routine pattern of set jobs: first, washing-up tea things, washing the little ones and putting them to bed; then our sewing hour when Miss Langley would read to us while we mended, darned and patched. Sometimes we helped to make new garments, but were only allowed to do easy parts like tacking or sewing on buttons. The eldest girls could use the one sewing machine in the afternoon when it was quiet.

To end the day, and one of the pleasurable tasks I was given, was to read aloud passages from the Bible; this was followed by prayers and 'doing the marks' for the day. Then we would go up to wash at the long washstand in the dormitory. Before we got into bed, matron would come up and we had to say a text and short prayer. If matron was not in, Dorothy would deputise and always seemed slightly embarrassed by this duty.

If we were a bit later than usual and had to hurry with the ablutions, matron would say, 'Just a lick and promise tonight'. Once I asked her, 'A promise of what?' and she replied, 'Of less next time'. I always thought this very funny; I still prefer it to the more accepted version - 'of more next time'.

Other days had their appointed tasks. Tuesdays was the day for ironing if the washing was dry enough. This was done in the kitchen. The old flat irons had to be heated on the range which, like the copper fire and most domestic stoves, was subject to direction of wind and the state of the chimney. On a good-tempered day this was a comparatively pleasant job. My fault was taking too long doing it: the kitchen was warm and cosy to work in; seeing each garment becoming smooth and neatly folded and sweet smelling gave a sense of satisfaction. Even the view of the back yard was a change. Sometimes one would see a tradesman come with a box of groceries, or the baker bring long loaves of bread. Naturally we never used the bread the day it arrived; it was stored on high shelves in the pantry. Generally two loaves would be joined together; one day a mouse popped out of the part where the loaves joined. Two whole loaves could not be wasted so a portion was cut away and the rest used. Loaves were larger than they are nowadays.

Wednesday was the day for a less appealing job: scrubbing the stairs which were not carpeted - just bare wood. In my opinion this task was a waste of time; somehow the bare wood did not respond to our efforts. How mad we would get if someone found it necessary to go up or down while we were still scrubbing. We had to wear a course apron made of stiff thick hession for tasks like this. How I disliked it - there was a sort of poverty-striken look about it. One felt like a work-house inmate in it. Woe betide any girl who was careless enough to leave a bucket or bar of carbolic soap unattended, even for an instant. It does not need much imagination to fortell the dire consequences should someone use the stairs and not expect to find an obstacle thereon: the stairway was not very well lit.

On Thursday the small rooms would have their share of cleaning - the little bedroom at the top of the stairs where Dorothy slept with one of the little ones in a cot, then the bathroom and lavvy.

On Friday, the big dormitory had to be thoroughly cleaned. Everything, apart from beds, had to be moved into the centre of the room; all clothes-baskets were well washed, potties scrubbed and their rather odd looking yellowish lids - like papier mâché plates - were replaced. The whole floor had to be washed with soapy water, on hands and knees, and wiped as dry as possible. Pails of water were carried up and down the stairs to be emptied and refilled about four times by each of the two girls on the job. It did look nice when it was finished and everything was put back tidily.

Matron's bedroom and the kitchen were done by the senior girls. At spring-cleaning time, china and other oddments which adorned a huge dresser along almost the whole side wall of the kitchen and never seemd to be used, was taken down and washed, piece by piece in the scullery sink. Some of the larger dishes were quite heavy and any girl, perched rather precariously on the wide part of the dresser, heaved a sigh of relief as the dish was passed safely down to another girl, who took it to be washed. Then the whole dresser was scrubbed and the china was not replaced until it was quite dry; it was a lengthy process.

The weather determined when windows should be cleaned. I have no recollection of the long curtains in the school room ever being washed or cleaned, but it stands to reason that they had to be done sometimes.

The chimney of the kitchen range had to be swept periodically and for days afterwards everything seemed to smell of soot, however carefully we cleaned up when the sweep had left. When he came to sweep the chimney in the school room we were allowed to watch for the fuzzy flat-topped brush to appear from the top of the chimney, outside. If the sweep was not in a great hurry he would give it a saucy twirl, especially to amuse the little ones. The range also had to be cleaned with blacklead brushes carried in a wooden box with a handle over the top. The blacklead came in a block about four inches by two inches; it was soaked with water and vinegar overnight to make a paste for use in the morning: it gave a good shine.

An unpleasant task fell to my lot shortly after I left school. I was put in charge of five or six girls who had contracted the distressing symptoms of ringworm. This was not uncommon and was probably caught from other girls at school; cleanliness was not on every family's priority list. Rings of sores and scurf appeared on the head causing bare patches and intense irritation in the hair. This happened in the early days of medical examinations by Health Officers and Nurses who visited schoools to seek out any pupils with head-lice or ringworm. A new form of treatment was being used at the clinic in Poole and our group had to attend twice a week. We had to walk all the way there, about three miles, and back, unless it was a very wet day and then we could go on a tram.

I am not certain what form the treatment took but I remember it involved electricity. It affected the girls in different ways: some would feel sick at the sight of food, some had faint blue weals across their backs although they did not seem painful. Their hair had to be shaved close to the scalp and a strong smelling red ointment rubbed in. Every child treated in this way had to wear a white cotton bonnet night and day, with a fresh one put on every morning. All infected girls were kept from school but not isolated from the rest of us at home. Why these bonnets, made from part-worn sheets, had to be washed in disinfectant and hot water with carbolic soap, I can only put down to economy; but it was my job to wash these horrid greasy objects and I hated it. I was more than thankful when the epidemic died out and I was not needed to do this supervising and washing any more.

The effect of the treatment on one little maid was truly startling: she was only about six years old and rather plain with mousy-coloured hair and a careworn, anxious, prematurely aged look on her face. Some weeks after the electrical treatment, her hair appeared in soft, silky curls all over her head, completely transforming her into a bright laughing maiden with quite merry eyes and a ready smile: she began to look more like a happy child again. She was younger than me - I have often wondered where the paths of her life have led her.

As we grew older we were allowed to let our hair grow. I had forgotten how long it grew until I was suprised to see the length of mine in a photo which I unearthed recently: I am sitting in a cradle-shaped seat with a doll: which had been given to St. Faiths by a young lady who had outgrown her treasure. It was called Violet after the donor, and there was a complete set of clothes, and a cot fully-equipped with bed clothes. I do not know why I had to have my photograph taken with the doll - I was not a 'dolly' sort of girl - but the photograph was probably taken for a Christmas present for my mother and sisters.

Once I made three hemstitched hankies for them with real drawn-threadwork all around the hem. No doubt they were not very neat: the corners were difficult to do. I like to think they were treasured by my family. They used to send me lovely toys for birthday and Christmas gifts. My favourite was a grey fur squirrel which had a thick tail which was silvery like a pussy willow catkin. When one of the girls at school became very ill and had to go to hospital we were asked to bring some toys for her. In a high-minded moment I parted with my treasure. When she died I would have liked to ask for it back; but of course I could not. I only hoped some other sick child would love it too.

After about three years I wore my hair scraped severely back away from my face into a bun at the back. I used to envy girls who had fine, wavy or curly hair - it was easier to manage. Mine had been curly when I was very young but years of constant cutting resulted in a wiry harsh mass of almost black unmanageable hair. No matter how many long steel hair-pins I used, before the morning was over they had sprung out and left an untidy raggle-taggle sprouting out like a demented halo. It was ages before my hair became softer and more manageable.

Our only shampoo was green slimy-soft soap, the same as we used for some household cleaning jobs. This concoction frothed and foamed all over the place and was an awful job to rinse out completely. One of my real secret ambitions was to have auburn hair, but like other hopes, it did not happen.

We were also given permission to wear clothes other than the Home uniform. We had the pick of clothes that were sent in for jumble sales and great was the excitement when, under the supervision of Dorothy, we were invited to choose from the pile spread out on the schoolroom table. Each girl could only have a limited number of garments and we had to pay for them ourselves. Even if some needed alterations done we were well pleased with our bargains and trying on the clothes resulted in fun for all.

When the time came for me to leave the Home for employment else where, my departure was delayed. It was quite a shock to discover that Dorothy felt in need of a change herself and had found other suitable employment. We all liked her and clubbed together to give her a parting present as well as several home-made efforts of our own.

The problem of getting a new assistant matron could not be solved immediately; I was by this time the eldest girl and so took on the position until someone suitable could be found. It was not by any means an easy job. Natually, I did not have the authority to give orders or to 'boss' the other girls. The hours were long; often I would be too tired to wash before going to bed and used to leave my clothes in an untidy heap on a chair beside the bed. I was given the privilege of sleeping in the little room at the top of the stairs; this meant I had to comfort any of the little ones who were not well, who would sleep in the blue cot in this room until they were better.

I filled this position for several months and my pay was 2/6d a month. Eventually Mrs Phillips became the successful applicant; she had a daughter, Freda, at St. Faiths.

A recollection nudges my mind at this point. During the time I stayed on until Mrs Phillips was familiar with the running order of things, she would have a half-day free once a week. One day she invited me to go to Mudeford to see her friends. In those days, Mudeford was in Hampshire but because of a change in county boundaries Mudeford, Christchurch and Highcliffe are now allocated to Dorset. It is only a few miles from where I am now living.

On the occasion of the outing I remember seeing men fishing in a river mouth; on the opposite bank they drew up a large net with very few fish in it. It was quite fascinating. I did not know then that this is a region famous for its salmon. Then I was taken to a small cottage nearby. It was rather dark inside. I was impressed most by a small writing bureau. I watched the man of the house go over to it and take out a pen and some paper. From that moment on, I longed for a bureau of my own. It was many years before I actually possessed one.

Eventually, in March 1919 after 12 years at the Home, I was accepted into the home of three women who lived at Lilliput, Sandbanks. I was to start work as a 'tweeny' - a between maid. Before leaving St. Faiths I had to be kitted out for my entry into private domestic service. Oh, that I had a photograph of myself in my new outfit. I hardly dare describe the agonies of getting into a corset. The ones I had been wearing needed replacing, so brand new ones were provided. None of today's Comfort Figure Control, super lightweight creations; these were thick, harsh material, reinforced with strips of whalebone and steel busks about five or six inches long let into the front of the corset with a eye and pop arrangement. With the constant bending of scrubbing floors these would snap and the sharp edges dug into my flesh: I wonder that I do not have a permanent scar on my tummy. They made holes in my vests too, and it needed patience to replace a broken pair instead of buying a whole garment.

The back of the corset had a kind of white shoelace to fasten the two halves of the garment together - no wonder it was often likened to armour plating. To start with, I had no pretensions to a waistline at all: as one girl said, I was like a sausage. You can imagine the agony of trying to get encased in this contraption and still leave enough freedom for movement.

The costume I was supplied with, not of my choosing, was designed for an elderly body. It was a peculiar and most unflattering shade of yellow-green, heavy material. The skirt was very long, reaching to my ankles with a silky fringe round the hem. The jacket had a nipped-in waist - which I had not - so the buttons had to be left undone. The blouse was made of pretty floral delaine material - a very fine, soft woollen fabric, a shade too small for me. My plump figure stretched it to bursting point and the sleeves were skin-tight on my fat arms. Even then my muscles were well-developed.

The crowning glory was a potty-shaped black felt hat with a band of orange-coloured corded-ribbon round it and a shaded feather sticking up almost in the front. My feet were encased in a pair of substantial black lace-up walking shoes with stockings of lisle, the fashion of the day.

Early one afternoon in March, one of the ladies for whom I was going to work came to fetch me in a pony trap. Goodness knows how she controlled her amusement at the quaint figure waiting for her. After goodbyes had been said and lots of advice given, my battered tin box was hoisted into the trap. I climbed up feeling scared and lonely as Kitty trotted off, bearing me along the road to my new life.

Dorset and Paddington

I arrived at Valley House to begin my duties as a between-maid. Miss Bottomley took me to the back door and rang the bell; it was opened by the cook, Nellie, and Miss B. introduced us. Then I carried my battered tin box which contained all my worldly goods into the kitchen. Nellie showed me upstairs to change into my new uniform before meeting the rest of the staff. I was only too glad to get out of the peculiar clothes I had been wearing. Afraid of being too long and yet dreading to meet strangers, I made as much haste as I could. I managed to loosen the corset which restricted my every movement; then I tidied my unruly hair. Thank goodness, I looked a bit more normal in a dark-blue dress and crisp white apron with a cap perched precariously on my hair.

I found my way down the stairs where Nellie was waiting for me in the kichen. She was middle-aged and had a kindly smile. She said she hoped we would work well together; she took me to the servant's hall to meet the rest of the staff. The parlourmaid, Barton, looked very smart in her black dress and spot-muslin apron and fancy-style cap. The housemaid, Allen, who had been at Valley House for several years seemed rather older than the other two and had a stern manner. Allen and Barton were always known by their surnames.

As the new girl, my first job was to clear the tea-table and wash the tea-things. The cook showed me where to put everything away: china in the cupboards and tablecloth in a drawer. I was too nervous to notice much of my surroundings or enjoy the meal. The washing up was done in the kitchen some distance away from this room.

I went up to unpack my few belongings and take stock of the room which I was to share with Barton. Nellie and Allen had separate rooms. All these rooms were on the third storey and had a lovely view across Poole Harbour.

Later, Nellie - who was not considered old enough to be addressed as 'Mrs': a courtesy title usually given to cooks and housekeepers - said that if I wished I could help her prepare the evening meal. Although my work did not start officially until the morning, I decided it would be useful to get some idea of what was expected of me. Preparations for the three-course dinner began at 6.30 and the food was ready to serve at 8.00.

I did not meet my new employers until the following morning; the eldest of the three maiden sisters was Miss Mia, who was gentle and ladylike in every way. She attended to the flowers around the house and consulted the gardener every morning. Miss Edith was more brisk and businesslike; she took an interest in local affairs and later became a magistrate. She also undertook the care of the hens which supplied eggs and meat for the household; and when a fowl needed to be killed she did the necessary. The third sister, Miss Mollie, was in charge of all housekeeping and domestic affairs. Each morning she would visit the kitchen to plan the day's menus and attend to the ordering of groceries and supplies. These ladies looked after their staff well and were proud that their servants were loyal and usually stayed for years. The 'tweenies', as between-maids were called, would not stay as long; they moved after two or three years to gain more experience and better themselves.

In a cottage near the front entrance to the drive lived a gardener, his wife and their two sons. Mr and Mrs May were a homely couple and we became good friends. Mr May was a conscientious gardener, the results of his labours bore witness to this: the flower beds and herbacious borders were a delight at all seasons, while the kitchen garden was a model of neatness and produced a variety of vegetables to supply every culinary need. There was also an enclosed area for soft fruits, apples and pear trees where no bird dare venture.

Mr May came to the kitchen for his daily orders from the cook and returned with fruit and vegetables as required which he would always place carefully on the table. One day he watched me peeling swedes or turnips - rather wastefully he thought. I felt conscious of him standing there; he told me off for wasting his precious vegetables and had to be pacified by Nellie who explained that one could not peel these vegetables thinly like potatoes: the skin had to be cut inside a fibrous line or they would be spoilt in the cooking.

My daily routine began at 6.30am. The first job was to attend to the cooking range which had been slacked up overnight with small coal, damped down with tealeaves and other waste. It needed raking out; the dampers were opened which caused the fire to burn up. Once a week the flues had to be cleaned which meant getting up half-an-hour earlier. It was quite a goodtempered range and I soon learnt to manage it. At 7 o'clock I took a cup of tea up to Nellie and had one myself between jobs: sweeping and dusting the servant's hall, laying the breakfast table and helping Nellie prepare breakfast for the servants which had to be cleared away before the ladies meal was ready at 9 o'clock.

During the morning I was under the supervision of Allen. My work upstairs consisted of making beds, sweeping and dusting the ladies' bedrooms, tidying and cleaning the wash basins in each room and emptying the chamber-pots which were kept in small cupboards by the bedside. The least popular job was cleaning the three copper hot-water cans. This was done in the staff bathroom which also contained linen cupboards and a chest of drawers: the top of this was useful as a working surface. Woe betide me if a smear or a dark line of tarnish was left unpolished. Once I had to use some rancid polish: the awful smell affected my throat and made me feel ill. At first Allen took no heed of my complaints but later she did produce a fresh tin for me to use.

Allen was a stickler for punctuality and precisely at noon I had to return to the kitchen and unfinished work had to be completed in my spare time at the end of the afternoon. From midday until bedtime, kitchen work was the order of the day. A myriad jobs clamoured for my attention: scouring pots and pans, preparing vegetables, scrubbing tables and cleaning floors, laying out utensils for the cook, keeping the fire up and the hearth and fender clean. At least, after the washing up was done and everything was left tidy, I could have a few quiet minutes. I changed out of my print dress, which was a morning or working dress, to the navy-blue one, and put on a clean white apron: I took a special pride in these stiff aprons although they were not as dainty and attractive as the ones worn by Barton but were practical and neat and suited my homely status.

At one time the house- and parlourmaids had plain black dresses with pretty white aprons and dainty caps. One day, a surprise awaited them: they were called into the drawing-room and presented with lovely blue dresses and caps with matching velvet ribbons threaded through an embroidered band. Although I envied and admired their new outfits, I had no desire to undertake duties which would take me to the front of the house. I could never have waited at table or served the gentry of whom I was really scared; I was content to keep out of their way and get on with the humbler tasks.

The house was always kept up to a very high standard, both inside and out. Periodical examination of every part was carried out at least once a year. Paintwork was touched up, window frames and catches were examined and tested and spring roller blinds, curtains, fittings, carpets and upholstery all had their share of attention. Outside walls had the roughcast whitened, brickwork was repointed and gutterings and drains cleaned. Chimneys were swept whether much used or not, all carpets were sent away to be cleaned and repaired if they showed signs of wear. Blankets and bedlinen, table cloths and linen from the store cupboard, had been thoroughly turned out and fresh paper put on the shelves.

I completed one year in service quite happily and by this time had earned an annual holiday which had to be arranged to suit the ladies' convenience. I went to visit my mother and sisters who were living in a small flat in Kensal Green, in North London and spent a pleasant time getting to know more about them.

I had been back at work for some time when a peculiar disease came to Valley House: all four maids became victims of the distressing complaint called scabies or the 'itch'. It was a mystery how this condition could have been present in such an immaculately kept house. The doctor was summoned; each one of us was examined and embarrassing and intimate questions were asked each of us separately. We were isolated from outside contacts and not allowed to visit friends and relations for the quarantine period. We were requested not to let anyone know of this condition. It was an unmentionable disease. The treatment was severe and time-consuming: each day we had a bath as hot as we could stand and we used a special soap which had to be rubbed well into the skin. Modesty had to be set aside as we had to help each other. A fair amount of extra work was caused: all towels needed rinsing after every bath. After about three weeks the problem ended due to our rigorous and drastic treatment.

In a subtle way I was made to feel that I had brought the disease back with me from my mother's home - although I was the last one to catch it. One of the ladies proposed going to see the district and conditions of housing in which she lived. I became the scapegoat and suffered a great deal of mental agony and spent sleeplesss nights over the problem. I resented the implications and the coldness of the other maids; we had all been friendly until then and I had been quietly happy in my work. If I had had more courage I would have given in my notice but I wondered if I would be given a reference. There was no chance of changing employment without that vital scrap of paper - a summary of one's character and ability.

Eventually life returned to normal but it was a long time before a relaxed atmosphere was fully restored. Strangely, the ladies were unaffected by the disease.

My free-time was limited to one half-day a week and every other Sunday afternoon. In the summer I had to be in by 10 o'clock and by 9.30 during the winter. Most of my free-time was spent cycling or roaming round the countryside. In the summer I would often spend hours on the beach at Sandbanks. I was content to walk along the shore taking in the natural beauty around me. I never ventured into the water or learnt to swim: I think I was afraid to leave my clothes in a pile unattended on the beach in case they were stolen or hidden. So I would sit in the sun and read or doze. One day, as I sat up everything seemed to swim around me and I felt sick and faint. When I recovered I strolled down to the sea and dabbed my face with water which refreshed me; I learnt never to sit in bright sun without some shade nearby.

The first bicycle I owned was sent to me by my mother. It was a sturdy affair with a padded seat: this caused some amusement and remarks were passed about my own seat being already well-padded. That bicycle became a valuable friend to me. I would cycle to Poole which was considered an economical shopping centre. I spent hours searching for bargains: once I bought some yellow dusters for ¾d each.

During fine weather I liked to walk along Poole Quay or sit and watch vessels from other countries arrive and depart. The place had an interesting smell of tar, ropes and the sea. Small fishing boats and ferries to Brownsea Island would come and go; there was always some movement to watch. In winter I would stay out until dusk; then I would go up to my room and read or write letters, sitting on a chair resting the pad on my knees; there was no heating and my hands would get very cold. One day Nellie asked me why I sat there alone and told me that I could use the servants' hall when off-duty; this made a lot of difference: it was warm and I was given permission to use the sewing machine to make my own clothes. I was a good needlewoman and enjoyed mending, darning, patching and general repairs.

After two years, Nellie decided to leave to spend more time with her semi-invalid father. Her replacement, Lavinia, was an excellent cook who taught me much, which gave me a certain amount of confidence. I was allowed to make the daily batch of scones. Lavinia was as short in stature as I was, but was able to wear high-healed shoes on her dainty feet, which I envied. She wore her thick hair piled up high giving her a slightly top-heavy look. She had a very economical nature and always spotted a bargain for household use. One July she bought up several yards of unbleached twill cotton sheeting in the White Sales at a large department store. She hoped to make this into sheets to use after her marriage but sadly the engagement was broken off and she left.

Another change took place when Barton left to get married. The new parlourmaid and I did not hit it off; it was not long before we had one difference of opinion and she gave in her notice. She said she was leaving because whe was not used to working with a 'charity girl'. I was very angry when I overheard this and gave in my notice too; it was most unusual for two servants to give notice at the same time. We gave our reasons individually to all three ladies; they refused to accept my notice as I had been working satisfactorily for two years. The parlourmaid had to leave and although I felt a certain sense of guilt I was happier after she had gone.

Life went on evenly for some time until a few months later I suffered from 'flat-feet' - a condition often met with scornful amusement. For some time I kept quiet about the pain in my feet which was more noticeable after sitting, than standing up; the soles of my feet seemed to be on fire. One evening cook came into the kitchen and saw me attempting to wash-up by kneeling on the seat of a chair drawn up to the front of the sink. I was unaware of her and she fetched the other maids who peeped at me through the serving hatch. They all laughed at me but soon realised that something was really wrong. The ladies were duly informed and I was advised to go and see my panel doctor. After cycling the four-mile journey I found I could scarcely stand. I must have looked very woebegone when I entered the surgery. The doctor advised me to take three weeks complete rest with my feet up; he realised the difficulties that this would entail and so said he would inform my employers. It was getting dark by the time I cycled back and I dared not stop to light the acetylene lamp. When I returned I was told to stay in bed until the doctor came in the morning. That night I could not sleep but puzzled my brain as to where I could go for three weeks. However, after consultation between doctor and the ladies, it was decided that I would have to stay where I was. Once again I had to face a barrage of questions and felt very awkward to cause so much trouble: someone had to bring my meals up two flights of stairs and bring me two bowls of water - one hot, one cold, in which I had to plunge my feet for ten minutes each, as part of the treatment. Sometimes Mrs May would come up and chat with me.

About three weeks later Miss Edith came up for a serious discussion: she said I was living on their charity and could I not go home to my mother, or perhaps even return to St. Faiths. However justified they may have been, I doubt if she alised how deeply her words hurt; it seemed servants were t supposed to have any feelings. The only solution was to before the doctor and be signed off the panel and hope that nature would heal me herself. For years afterwards I wore heavy metal arch supports and lace-up boots in summer and winter.

One of my regular jobs was to take letters to the nearest post-box which I did in my free-time after tea and before preparing the evening meal. It was an enjoyable walk; sometimes I would return a long way round noting the wayside flowers and the scent of pine trees on a warm summer evening. A certain clump of pine trees was, according to local legend, the site of a gallows and was still called Gallow's Copse or Gallow's Corner.

After about two and a half years I felt I had absorbed as much as I could as a between-maid. General housework did not interest me as much as working in the kitchen and cooking. I also felt it was time I became better acquainted with my mother and sisters. Each week I studied the Church Times which the housemaid passed on to me. One day I answered an advertisement requiring a kitchen-maid for a residence in Paddington. I knew nothing of the geography of London but by looking at a map of Paddington it did not seem too far away from Kensal Green.

I was offered the job and I began a new style of life as a kitchen-maid; the house was a tall building in Southwick Crescent, Paddington, and the master was a colonel abroad in the army; if I remember correctly his full military title was Brevet Lieutenant Colonel Ebeneezer Lecky Pike; he was described as the most handsome man in the British Army. Even though this new position was considered a step up from a between-maid, I joined the humblest place in the ranks of the staff which consisted of a lady's maid, nanny, nursemaid, house-parlourmaid, cook and myself. When the Colonel was in residence his batman joined the staff. The Colonel's wife, Mrs Pike, was a well-known society hostess and artist. She was reputed to have the slimmest, trimmest ankles. She frequently held dinner parties and supervised the menu on these occasions. They had two children.

My duty was to assist Mary, the cook - an Irish woman with an enviable complexion in spite of working in a semi-basement. She was kind but not so thorough in minor matters as the cooks I had been used to working with. I also had to clean the front door-step, bell and letter-box. As I stood in the basement all I saw of passers-by was their feet hurrying along the pavement.

One day, I was aware of a pair of feet near me but inside the hall. Then I noticed a pair of bright yellow pyjamas with black cats romping over them in all attitudes. They were worn by Col. P. He muttered something and moved away.

Mary attended mass every Sunday and after a while I had to be responsible for Sunday breakfasts for the dining room and nursery staff. The mistress did not get up for breakfast and so a tray had to be sent up to her bedroom.

It was a fairly hundrum existence, enlivened now and then by some trivial incident: one such happening was while Mary was preparing a clear soup for a dinner party. Calamity struck when the eggshells, used to clarify the consommé, stuck to the bottom of the saucepan spoiling both colour and flavour. Mary was distraught: she wrung her hands and cried, 'Mercy on us, I am undone, I am destroyed'; this was her favourite saying when in distress. Suddenly, as I was quietly attending to the vegetables, she told me to go upstairs and fetch her rosary which hung on the wall above her bed. I climbed four flights of stairs and returned cautiously as I was unable to hurry down stairs since my foot-trouble days; I was roundly scolded for being a long time. She snatched it from me, kissed it and then plunged it three times into the soup with muttered incantations. I was stunned into silence and almost burnt the potatoes. A minor miracle was wrought as no complaint reached the kitchen; next morning the mistress complimented Mary on the dinner and remarked on the delicate flavour of the soup.

One day Mary made a strange remark which has stuck in my mind ever since; she said that the Prince of Wales would never be crowned King of England, although at this time he was at the peak of his popularity. When he returned after one of his world travels he was met with a triumphant welcome home. We stood on a narrow balcony to watch the procession pass: I remember seeing His Royal Highness give his famous smile and salute; he was dressed in naval officer's uniform. I was surprised by his youthful appearance and the fairness of his hair. The mistress had painted a portrait of him and she placed this right opposite the door of her studio.

After I had settled into my new situation I decided to write to mother; I would like to have given her a surprise by unexpectedly walking in one day but decided against this. I began to visit them fairly regularly although my limited free- time was not always convenient for them. So I would first visit a museum but I was too shy to ask the attendants any questions - what a wealth of knowledge I missed. Then I ould arrive at mother's at tea-time and she would have a ch of viota cakes for tea.

I enjoyed riding across London by bus; if I could, I ays sat in a front seat on the top deck which gave a ely view of many unseen parts of the town; it was exciting to be on a level with the branches of trees and I'd instinctively duck when they brushed against the windows. It was fascinating to note the changing growth in all seasons: in springtime the opening of fresh foliage on twigs and branches, with buds swelling more each time I passed, into full green leaves; and many kinds of flowers which were not easily seen when walking below. In autumn there would be a lavish display of colour and finally, after the leaves had fallen, the intricate pattern of bare branches could be seen: the different shapes of buds and twigs giving each tree its own distinctive outline.

Sometimes my eldest sister would take me to a cinema; on another occasion mother took me to Regents Park Zoo. When I arrived at her house she said that my hat was not fashionable enough and so persuaded me to borrow one of my sister's: it was a navy-blue felt hat trimmed with a plait of small irridescent beads which ended in a bugle - a fairly long tassel which hung down to one side - I felt very swish. I found it interesting, my first sight of so many animals. I felt sorry for the lions and tigers - such handsome huge creatures with sad peculiar eyes pacing to and fro in small cages. We waited for feeding time and stood with other people outside the cage. A dark foreign lady approached one of the tigers and stroked the bars of the cage; the tiger came towards her and made a curious rough purring sound and rubbed his head along the bars; he extended a paw and the woman spoke quietly in gibberish. When the keeper's trolley could be heard approaching she seemed to glide away without a sound. My mother wondered if she belonged to a circus.

At the monkey house my sister's hat received a shower from one of the inmates. We tried to remove the marks when we returned home but were unsuccessful; so the hat was put back in its box and nothing was said. It was many years before my sister learned what had caused the spots.

Another favourite place to spend an hour or two was Kensington Gardens. Nannies would congregate there and chat together while their charges became engrossed in sending their boats across the water. No doubt many were dreaming of becoming famous explorers and intrepid sailors. Elderly gentlemen would also enjoy fun with their cronies racing superb models of sailing ships.

I may not have benefitted from visits to museums but I did learn how rich folk put on a good appearance without spending too much money. When a society hostess wanted to impress her guests at a dinner party she would have certain 'items on approval' for the evening or a few days, such things as crystal table-ware, a specially handsome vase for a table centre-piece, a beautiful chandelier or a good quality dinner service or delicate china coffee set. Small dinner parties would be arranged for two or three nights in succession. After a few days the goods would be returned to the store. Sometimes clothes would be sent out 'on appro'. On one occasion things did not go according to plan; it was the tennis season and a tennis dress had been ordered. However after a strenuous game it showed obvious signs of having been worn and not merely tried on for effect: the fashion house refused to accept it back and so it had to be paid for.

Another near disaster concerning a gown comes to mind: Mrs Pike was painting the portrait of a beautiful foreign princess; she would visit the studio on certain days for a sitting and one day a stolen glimpse through the open door gave me a fleeting picture of a lady in a deep midnight-blue flowing gown. Mrs Pike suggested to the princess that she should leave this gown at the studio and that Muriel, the lady's maid, would assist her in changing into it before each sitting. She agreed to this and so Pike instructed Muriel to make a copy of the robe. In order to do this much unpicking and sewing together was needed. Then one day the princess's own personal maid called in a chauffeur-driven car to collect the gown which was unexpectedly needed for some special occasion. Unfortunately Muriel had not finished stitching it up and an excuse had to be made: they said that the garment was in a locked wardrobe and that the Lady's maid had the key and was not at home. Fortunately this explanation seemed to work and the visiting maid arranged to call back later. What panic the frantic needlewoman must have felt as she hastily machined and pressed the seams. Eventually, however, it was collected and no comment was made. This incident was a topic of great interest among the downstairs staff.

During the summer the family combined with three or four related families for a holiday by the sea; a school on Hayling Island was rented for six weeks and several servants from each family were taken to make up the staff: housekeeper and lady's maid from one, parlourmaid and housemaid from another, and the housekeeper's son and myself and a chauffeur. There were about twenty people to cater for, including children and nannies which meant that my hands were seldom idle. The fresh sea air, bathing and other activities gave them plenty of appetite; it seemed that meals needed preparing from breakfast to late supper. Lashings of ham, cold roast beef, lamb and corned beef were always on hand; as well as brawn and home-made galantines. Salads galore, potatoes enough to feed an army and many other vegetables all had to be ready to serve in a matter of minutes at any time of day:

the families would drift in at odd hours and expect to be served. One day the housekeeper put her foot down and said the situation could not continue as it was unfair to the limited kitchen staff. She said that we were not running a hotel and that people who were not punctual could not expect instant attention. The situation improved and life became easier.

I remember how I was tempted one day by a large yellow bowl of prunes which was kept on a shelf in the pantry; I passed it many times a day and could not resist them. Never did I tire of them nor did they seem to affect my inner-man! Having nowhere handy to put the stones I would pop them into my apron pocket wrapped in odd bits of paper. One day when I received my apron back from the laundry a note was pinned on the garment: 'please remove contents of pocket before sending to the laundry' - complete with the stones in a neat packet!

The aroma of mint sauce will always evoke memories of the large quantities I had to make while on that holiday; many idle moments were spent washing and chopping mint - sugar was added to make the chopping easier; this mixture was put into a cup with a drop of boiling water to help keep the colour, then stirred well with enough vinegar to make a blend thick enough to be held in a spoon - a silver spoon was used to prevent a metallic taste.

Very occasionally I found time to wander down to the beach; the house was so near that folk could walk down in their bathing gear and leap straight into the briny: it was unusual then for people to expose much of their bodies. And thereby hangs a tale. One day as I was passing through the kitchen to the servants' hall I noticed the chauffeur looking at some snapshots and showing them to another chap. I was curious and asked if I could see them but the men drifted away mumbling something about having things to do. Later I asked one of the other servants if she had seen them and she blushed and looked awkward. By now I sensed that something vaguely connected with me was going on. Eventually someone said I would find copies on the beach photographers board outside his hut. Determined to solve the mystery I sallied forth later that evening. The photographer was just packing up but I had time to see the mystery snaps: there I was large as life lying asleep on the beach with more of my feminine curves exposed than I would have dared to show had I been awake. Above the photographs was a caption: The Belle of Hayling. I was disgusted and furious but did not have the nerve to demand that he withdraw the pictures. I stormed at the chauffeur and made him fetch his copies and tear them up. A few days later he tried to kiss me; he said he liked the way my eyes blazed when I was angry. His reward was a slap in the face and after that he avoided me.

On one of my free Sunday evenings I went to church. Once I could not concentrate on the service: my attention was attracted by two sand fleas which were playing hide-and-seek inside the thin voile blouse of the lady in front of me. Her broderie anglais material was visible through the fine material and provided an excellent venue for their activities. I wondered if I should warn her but how could I say to a stranger, 'You have two fleas inside your blouse'? So off she went in ignorance.

The summer spent on Hayling Island provided a change but life soon went back to normal when we all returned to our homes. Life in Paddington went on much as usual until one day a letter arrived which was to provide an opportunity for change.

left, Edna aged 17 years, at Paddington,
wearing a light-blue sponge-cloth dress with a belt made with shiny beads and bugle, made by herself

right, Edna aged 19 years, at Chelsea,
wearing a navy dress

Chelsea

Since living in Paddington, I had occasionally visited Miss Grainge, former matron of St. Faiths who had retired to West Kensington where she had a flatlet. She would write to me inviting me to tea. I was made welcome: tea was served in fine china cups and she prepared lovely white bread and butter and dainty cakes. One day she wrote inviting me, and in her letter she hinted that she had some special news for me. After we had finished our tea she told me about a job as a kitchen-maid at the home of Sir Albert and Lady Gray in Chelsea which she felt would suit me more than my present position. I was very interested. After a successful interview I was offered the job and so handed in my notice to the Pikes.

My mother was pleased about the change, particularly as the job had been recommended by Miss Grainge and also because there was some prestige in working for titled gentry. Mother came with me to see the housekeeper, Miss Sheldon who assured her that I would be well looked after, provided I worked hard and kept clean and tidy. It was also made clear that I should treat her with respect. Mary gave me a writing compendium as a parting present and hoped I would write to tell her how my new life suited me.

I arrived at Catherine Lodge, Trafalgar Square, Chelsea on November 10th feeling more confident than in the past; I felt the position was a fortunate move for me. The house was lovely with an acre of ground and had been featured in Country Life. It was positioned between the Kings Road and the Fulham Road. The fire station was nearby and I remember the black horses which pulled the bright red fire-engine; it was said that when the fire-bell sounded the horses would stand in the right position for being harnassed.

At the rear of the house was a large garden with an ancient Mulberry tree in the centre of the lawn. Mrs Sheldon had been given permission to keep a few hens at the end away from the house; these used to lay enough eggs for table use. This was my first sight of newly-hatched chickens and I liked to be allowed to collect the eggs.

There was a pillar box on the pavement just outside the

back door. The regular postman was a miserable-looking chap and Emily, the under-housemaid, and I would see him coming from our bedroom window; sometimes we put odd items in the box to surprise him. One day we both dropped in a sprig of mistletoe attached to a Christmas card and we actually saw him smile - but we quickly popped back into the room away from the window before he could look up and see us.

A gardener came three times a week. Emily and I avoided him as his language was coarse and his ways sly. When he came in for mid-morning cocoa he would push past me - too close for my liking - to get to the roller-towel. Emily disliked him as he had once tried to kiss her. There was also a lady who came to help during spring-cleaning time. She was plump and jolly and cheered me up no end with her amusing stories. Once she found a gold sovereign among a bag of washing soda. It seemed that a shopkeeper in a general store in the part of Chelsea known as World's End, had spilt soda in his shop. He had swept it up along with a lost sovereign. It was such an amusing story I wrote it down and called it 'Two Pennyworth of Soda'. I sent it to a magazine but had no luck.

During my second morning, as I was lifting down a saucepan from a high shelf, I knocked some lids which fell with an awful clatter. Mrs Sheldon said crossly, 'You must stop that and be quiet': I thought she was scolding me for my clumsiness; then I head a 'boom, boom' and realised that I had unwittingly broken the two minutes silence which was observed on the eleventh hour of the eleventh day of the eleventh month to commemorate the signing of the Armistice at the end of the First World War, to allow silent prayer for all those who had lost their lives in the cause of freedom. Rather sad that this is not still observed.

Gradually I got to know the rest of the staff. I shared a bedroom with Emily, who worked with Ada the head-housemaid who was strict and stern. If our free-time coincided Emily and I would go out together and became quite good friends. She took me to visit her relations who lived nearby. Lady Gray had a personal maid and Mr Jennings was the butler - he was well built and looked the part perfectly. It seemed strange to me that I had to take his early morning cup of tea to his room on the ground floor. His chief pleasure was a daily 'bob each way' on the races and he was never ill-tempered even when he lost. John was the footman; although his surname was Quick he did not live up to it. He was good-looking with thick dark curly hair and was a bit sweet on Emily: sometimes they would go to the pictures together.

Sir Albert and Lady Gray, with whom I had little contact, were extremely good to their staff who usually remained with them for years. They were both very tall and slim and aristocratic-looking. I was first introduced to her Ladyship on the morning after my arrival. She spoke encouragingly about the work and said that I would learn more about cooking and management than I had done in previous posts. My first meeting with Sir Albert a day or two later was embarrassing: I was wearing a coarse hessian apron over my dress as I scrubbed the front door step. Suddenly I was startled to hear a quiet voice say, 'We have not met before, have we?' In my haste to get up from my knees I nearly knocked over the bucket of soapy water and I had nowhere to wipe my wet hands. I managed to stammer out ' Good morning Sir Albert'; he replied that he hoped I would be happy working there. Then he picked up his daily paper from the hall table and went away. Still feeling awkward I carried my bucket along the pavement to the area steps instead of going my usual way across the hall. Mrs Sheldon was very amused at my embarrassment and said I had been honoured by Sir Albert speaking to me. I did wish I had not been wearing that coarse apron which was the usual type worn by servants when doing menial jobs. It seemed to emphasize the menial tasks we had to do, and was to me a 'badge of poverty'. However, I found a way of making myself some more attractive ones. In those days flour and sugar were supplied in white bags of heavy white material, not as coarse as hessian. I persuaded Mrs Sheldon to let me have a couple to experiment with. The blue printed lettering on them could be erased when the bags were boiled and bleached in the sun. I boiled them hard in an old saucepan used for boiling pudding cloths and then lay them out to bleach in the sun. The material became almost white and with it I carefully made some better-looking aprons.

One thing I had already learnt to do was skin a rabbit and pluck and draw chickens and game birds. Some of the game birds had to be 'high' with maggots in the flesh before they were cooked. I felt very sad at having to pluck the breast feathers and long tail feathers of pheasants; they were so beautifully arranged in lovely patterns; I gave the long feathers to my mother who used them to adorn hats. When skinning a rabbit one had to be careful not to tear or break the skin and to remove the ears completely. I disliked gouging the eyes out and cleaving the rabbit's head open to get at the brain. It was not uncommon to have a pregnant animal to deal with and the foetus was given to the dogs or cats of the household. I had also to deal with an eggbound hen.

One of my regular duties was to light the kitchen fire, a large two-oven range, and blacklead it every day and sweep the flues once a week. When the sweep came on his twice-yearly visits I had to get up at four o'clock to open the back door to let him in. After that it was not much good returning to bed so I would sometimes creep into the servants' hall and have a read until he had finished, then I had to clean up after him. It was a filthy job: soot was so penetrating and the smell lingered for days. The kitchen floor had to be scrubbed every Friday. The heavy galvanised bucket needed changing about three times and it was hard on one's hands and knees as the floor was made of stone slabs. Washing soda was added to the water and a chunk of red carbolic or green soft soap from a tin was used on the scrubbing brush. Somehow there were always people who found it absolutely necessary to walk across the floor before it had a chance to dry. When Sir Albert and Lady Gray returned from a visit to Jamaica she brought back the outer husk of a coconut and suggested that this cut in half would make a suitable scrubbing brush. They were very difficult to grip with wet soapy hands so I tried to chisel out grooves to fit my fingers in. The thick coir made a horrible scratching sound on the stone but I had my orders to use it, so did not question why.

Another duty was to clean the kitchen table: this was so large that I had to divide it into quarters to reach across when scrubbing it every day. Mrs Sheldon's habit of groooming Lady Gray's two Pekinese dogs on the kitchen table after I had cleaned it made me rather cross. One day I spread newspapers over the half where she put the dogs and told her how thoughtless she was; I was trembling and on the point of tears and expected to be given my notice on the spot. However Mrs Sheldon said she understood my point and from then on put newspapers on the table in the scullery before grooming.

The work as a kitchen-maid was hard: I remember well the daunting task of keeping clean over fifty pots and pans, many of them copper. When the polished pans were returned to their shelves they glowed warmly but in damp or foggy weather they would very sooon become tarnished and dull. Pots and pans in daily use had to be carefully examined for any signs of wear: the slightest spot of copper showing through the inner lining of tin and the pan would be put aside. About twice a year all affected pans would be collected and taken to a tinsmith to be relined and would return bright and shining inside, although the outsides still had to be cleaned.

Difficult items to polish were the elaborate jelly moulds with awkward corners and ledges in the designs. This almost daily job of keeping the array of pans fit for use was very unkind to the hands. For some reason best known to herself, Mrs Sheldon would never let me use a cloth to apply the mixture of silversand, lemon juice and vinegar: it was rough and gritty to touch and was applied by rubbing it into the copper with the palms of the hands, which turned an unprepossessing shade of green. Then constant immersing in hot water gave them an added rawness. When the cold weather came the chaps on my hands were particularly bad; trying to grip the feathers of the game birds I was given to pluck brought tears to my eyes. The job would take much longer than it should so I would have to continue during my free afternoon. I tried many kinds of handcream to improve the condition of my hands; however, when the corners of each thumb split and bled I went to a chemist for advice. I was so ashamed of my hands that I waited until no-one else was in the shop. He examined them and suggested a preparation called Glymiel Jelly; he warned me that it would probably sting at first, but to encourage me he offered the first tube free and made me promise to use it regularly and wear gloves at night and to return for more if necessary. Gradually my hands began to show some improvement and I became a loyal customer at that chemist's shop: he was always kind and considerate and secretly I wondered if my own father may have been like him.

A cast iron stockpot was kept on the side of the range at all times; almost anything edible went into it to provide the base for soups and sauces. This piece of hardware would today be considered unhygenic and unsafe. It was deep with a large handle and a heavy lid which was clamped on. Once a week it would be emptied so that it could be cleaned. I tipped the contents through the sieve into a large yellow bowl; this had to be done whilst still very hot so that the grease did not settle on the sieve. It was a very awkward process: if I put the contraption on the draining board it would be too high for me to lift the hotpot up to tip it. I tried standing it in the sink which was a better level for me to reach. Sometimes the sieve would tip sideways and spill much of the stock down the sink. Then the horrible job of washing the greasy pot remained. At least there was a good supply of really hot water which was necessary to remove the thick grease which clung to the inside of the pot: it was a task I did not relish but it had to be done.

There were no short cuts or instant preparations in preparing food in those days. At Christmas time there would be extra guests staying in the house giving rise to lunch and dinner parties: I enjoyed the extra work involved. There were many puddings and mince pies to prepare as Lady Gray would distribute them to the poor of the district; these had to be made well in advance as they were better for keeping. Sir Albert and Lady Gray would come out to the kitchen to have a traditional 'stir and wish'; silver coins were put in and Mr

Jennings would bring the necessary brandy or other ingredients in his care to be added under the supervision of Mrs Sheldon. He would be very jovial and tease Emily and me by offering us a glass of something. The pies would be stored in large tins and kept in the cool pantry. The puddings were boiled in basins covered with a cloth; when cooled the first cloth was taken off and a clean one put on and knotted and the basins hung on strong hooks high enough to be out of the reach of any venturesome mice.

What piles of fruit had to be prepared: there were real luscious raisins - sticky and shiny and plump; currants and sultanas - black and golden brown, and each fruit easily identifiable one from another; and candied peel, large lumps of lime, lemon and orange with a coating of sugar, crisp and sweet; all these were delivered in thick blue paper bags which, when opened, let out an intoxicating smell which made one's mouth water. I willingly gave up hours of my free-time to prepare these ingredients for puddings and cakes. The currants and sultanas were cleaned by spreading them - half a bag at a time - on a large sheet of greaseproof paper or an old tea-cloth which had been sprinkled with plain flour. The fruit was rubbed in it and riddled in a wire sieve and all the stems and odd bits were cast out; the cleaned fruit was then stored in heavy glass jars ready for use. Raisins had different treatment: it took nearly an hour to stone one pound by hand; there would be at least four or five pounds to be dealt with. It was a time consuming process - and what did it matter if a few did not reach the finished pile. My method was to have a large flat meat dish ready to receive the finished fruit which had to be spread out to dry, a basin of hot water, frequently renewed, in which to dip my sticky fingers and a smaller basin for the stone. These were later added to the chicken feed. These preparations were not tedious: the kitchen was warm and I had the whole table to work on uninterrupted for an hour or so until it was time to prepare the evening meal. Old Tommy the black-and-white cat lay in front of one of the ovens purring contentedly. There was plenty of scope for my imagination to wander. Later, when all the preparations for the festive meals were complete I would be allowed a glimpse of the dining table set out specially for the occasion, beautifully arranged with bowls of flowers and some festive greenery around the dining room, and a sprig of mistletoe in a favoured spot.

A job I did not like so much was suet chopping. The butcher boy delivered the suet, driving the pony trap; he would come whistling down the area steps with a parcel of large lumps of creamy-pink suet. This had to be freed from the skin and chopped up very small. A formidable chopping knife was needed and plenty of plain flour to keep the suet from sticking to the knife, to itself and the board. This really was a tedious job. One day Mrs Sheldon said she was feeling too tired to cope and would do it later. Little Miss Eager-to-please decided to do her good turn for the day and spend her free after-tea hour getting on with the job. When the prepared pile of suet was discovered by Mrs Sheldon the expected praise and thanks were not forthcoming. Instead a quite severe scolding was meted out because I had grated the suet on a coarse grater instead of chopping it by hand. I had to do it all again after my evening work was finished. A good resolution gone wrong: ah well, one of life's lessons learned.

A rather strange job I had each morning was to stir the breakfast eggs whilst they boiled so that the yolks would remain in the centre of the eggs. If they did not they would be sent back to the kitchen and another would have to be prepared.

Making ice cream, with custard and cream, was a difficult business. First the freezer had to be prepared; small pieces of ice were chipped from a huge chunk which we bought from an ice-merchant or fishmonger. These pieces would then be packed round a wooden tub between layers of salt petre into which was positioned a bucket which fitted to a central pivot. Then the ice cream mixture was poured into the bucket, a stout lid was put on and a handle fixed. This was another job which made my hands ache with cold. The handle was turned until the mixture became stiff as the cream froze.

On one memorable occasion we were making ice cream for a dinner party; the wretched mixture would not freeze. I turned and turned the handle between doing other jobs: tending vegetables or stacking and heating plates for the different courses. Eventually, as it was nearly time for the sweet to be served I had to confess to Mrs Sheldon. We had to improvise in a way which was horrific to a real cook: we opened a tin and whipped some cream - although I was not trusted even to do that. After the crisis had past I was given a downright good wigging for not revealing my mistake earlier. It was discovered I had been too lavish with the strawberry jam so that it would never have frozen completely. The servants were a little surprised at being given this mixture for their suppers.

One sweet that I found very exciting, was plain ice cream, which was put into a bell-shaped mould; at the last moment before serving it was tipped from the mould and hot chocolate was poured over it. Mr Jennings would wait at the kitchen door and hasten in to the dining room before it melted.

Making aspic jelly was a most complicated affair. The base was calves foot jelly which was made from bones and then set to allow any impurities or fat to settle. When the fat had been removed the aspic had to be clarified, using some crushed egg-shells which had to be whisked together; and once again the jelly was poured off and left to set. When it became a clear, pale straw colour, it had to be warmed: an inch or two was poured into a flat-bottomed copper, tin-lined mould. Before it had set too hard tiny snippets of vegetables were placed carefully in a pattern on the semi-liquid, then left to set. These vegetables had been previously cut up and cooked in separate pans: young peas often bought out of season and French beans cut into diamond shapes provided the green; also - small squares of carrot, a few pieces of turnip, but not too much in case it did not remain a good white colour; potato was never used as it would turn sour. Each layer was allowed to set slightly before a new layer was poured in. No two layers should contain vegetables of the same colour and the pieces forming the design were not to be placed uniformly above those in the previous layer. To complete the picture wafer thin crisps, cut by hand and fried to a light golden brown, would be placed around a mound of finely mashed potato topped with sprigs of bright green parsley. For a few moments it did indeed look attractive but once the serving spoon was plunged in - hey presto, away went the pattern so laboriously made.

A rather satisfying though complicated dinner dish was roast pheasant served with all the trimmings; it smelt delicious.

One job I was not too keen on preparing was a certain fish recipe. This involved pushing raw fillets of fish through a wire sieve. This was then mixed with egg and cream; pepper and salt were added and the scallops of fish poached in tin moulds well greased with butter. Three or four of these quennels would be served on a hot silver dish with a shrimp sauce in a silver sauce boat. Sir Albert would manage to eat one or perhaps one and a half.

Raw beef sandwiches were another peculiar item: best beef would be spread on a board and flayed to make it tender, then scraped and mixed with seasoning; this unappetising mixture was then spread on wafer thin bread and butter and cut into tiny squares.

Sometimes Mrs Sheldon would despair of ever getting Sir Albert to eat enough to nourish his spare frame. She contrived to have a talk with his doctor who suggested, partly as a joke, that she should serve tripe and onions suitably disguised with a rich sauce with a posh French name on the menu card. This she did and to our amazement Mr Jennings reported that Sir Albert had eaten two small helpings. He then asked Mr Jennings the name of the new dish. Lady Gray had a slightly better appetite but because of some obscure internal trouble she had to be very careful with her own diet. It was no wonder that they were both very slim.

I was able to arrange for my mother to come and help with the preparing of vegetables and washing up. Her fares and a small wage were paid and she never left empty-handed. She particularly appreciated a basin of real beef dripping - so tasty and nourishing on hot toast.

I had a disturbing experience early one evening when I returned to the kitchen to open up the fire in the range and prepare everything for the housekeeper's use. The oven doors had been left open to freshen the oven while the heat was not too intense. Automatically I pulled out the damper to get the fire going and shut the oven doors. I then began preparing the vegetables for dinner. A little later I opened the door of the left-hand oven; I had no special reason to do this but a sixth sense must have been at work. I noticed something white in the dark interior; puzzled I put my hand in to investigate and felt something soft and furry. I went stone cold as I realised is was Tommy, the cat. Quickly and gently I drew the limp body out and carried the apparently lifeless body (wrapped in the rough oven cloth) to the back door. I stood at the top of the area steps and fetched a saucer of water to tempt him to drink. Leaving him outside with the door open I returned to my work but kept popping out to see if he had recovered and stroke his matted fur which had clung to him as I drew him out of the oven. When Mrs Sheldon came out and discovered what had happened I cried with fear and relief when I realised he was recovering. Mrs Sheldon gave him a spoonful of brandy to help revive him. You may be sure that I looked carefully into the oven each evening after this frightening experience.

Later when Tommy became ill with gravel in his waterworks we asked Lady Gray if we could contact a vet. She came immediately to the kitchen to see him and decided that a vet be sent for straight away. Dinner was delayed that night. After three weeks he returned fully recovered. This episode made me aware of Lady Gray's kindly nature.

Somehow we had heard talk of a secret passage which was supposed to lead down to the River Thames and had once been used by smugglers. One day when Sir Albert and Lady Gray were away, Emily, John and I decided to explore. Underneath the front entrance was a coal cellar into which an enormous mound of coal was tipped through the manhole outside the front gateway. In this cellar we discovered another passage which we decided to venture down. We took the precaution of donning heavy coats and took candles and matches. When we reached the opening of the passage we lit our candle: I remember how they guttered. John led the way; the candle flames cast peculiar shapes on the brick walls. We stumbled on for what seemed a fair way; the air was full of dust and there was a musty smell so that we held our noses but it made little difference. We started coughing and giggling. Presently John's candle flickered and went out. John tried to strike a fresh match but dropped the box. He wanted to go back but Emily and I teased him and said we wanted to go on; I do not think we did, but felt he should have more spirit. So we went on cautiously; I stumbled but did not drop my precious candle. The flames flickered; Emily let out an exclamation of disgust as she felt something brush past her: it could have been a bat or a downhanging cobweb. Our courage was failing us and as John went a few steps further he too felt something soft in front of him. We all held our candles high and ahead of us could see dimly what appeared to be curtains draped on each side of a doorway. From somewhere a gust of wind blew out two of the candles: this left only mine and not much left of that. We felt by this time that we had explored enough that day and decided to return. The others lit their candles from the dying flame of mine and we trapesed back to the entrance of the passage. Hoping fervently that we would not meet anyone we made our way to our bedrooms for a good wash before returning to the servants' hall and normal life. We never did know whether there had actually been curtains or if it was only a thick draping of cobwebs with the accumulated dust of centuries. When asked where we had been all the afternoon we said, 'For a walk.'

A regular caller at the house was a man who came to wind and regulate all the clocks. No-one else was ever allowed to touch them. If one unexpectedly stopped he would be sent for. He was tall and very smart with an upright military bearing. He thought a lot of himself and took his job very seriously.

When Sir A. and Lady G. went away the staff were put on 'board wages' - that is, we were paid a regular sum each week out of which we had to buy our own food. It was more economical to pool our resourses and live together. Conferences were held each week in the servants' hall to plan menus for the week and Mrs Sheldon would pay all bills. If any cash was left at the end of a month it was either shared out equally or a treat like a visit to a cinema or theatre was arranged.

If Sir A. and Lady G. were away for a long period the extra cash was kept and paid out on the last day making a worth-while bonus.

An amusing incident occured on the morning Sir A. and Lady G. left for their three-month winter cruise to Jamaica. Our period of freedom began as they drove off in a taxi. Suddenly they returend and Sir Albert announced that he had left a pair of spectacles behind which he could not do without. Frantic searching by all the front of house staff brought no result. And then, at last, John noticed that Sir A was wearing two pairs of glasses - one over the other. There were sighs of relief and some discreet laughter and once again they were on their way.

Shortly after their return from this trip I fell ill with tonsilitis. Lady Gray showed great kindness and sent me to bed. Later she came up to see me and brought with her a bottle of Cologne. She tipped some on her handkerchief which she then wrapped round my throat. Then she called the doctor who announced that I had a high fever. Everyone was very kind during that illness; it was very different from treatment I had received in earlier days. Later, however, I did hear that the lady's maid took a dim view of 'her' Lady Gray being so personal as to use one of her own handkerchiefs on 'a kitchen-maid's throat'.

Some excitement was caused when Sir Albert was elected Mayor of Chelsea. I could never quite understand how a quiet unassuming gentleman could have been chosen.

After two and a half years I felt that it was time to leave; I wanted to do more cooking and this was not possible to arrange without finding a new situation. I was sorry to lose my friends and old Tommy who seemed to know that something was amiss. As I sat waiting for the time to go he sat at the top of the area steps and came in now and then to rub against me. I arranged to return to Valley House, Lilliput, as cook. It turned out not to be the best of ideas, but I was by now a less unsure person and was beginning to stand on my own two feet.

New Beginnings

This time I arrived from the station in a taxi with a more respectable trunk and wearing a less quaint outfit than the one I had worn when I came from St. Faiths several years before. Kitty trotted a little less briskly and was a little plumper in her middle age. The three ladies greeted me kindly and hoped I would be happy and successful as the cook. They did not seem to have changed much; the house and garden were still well-kept. The gardener and his wife made me welcome and we renewed our friendship. There was some reluctance on the part of the older members of the staff, who remembered me from before, to accept me as cook - a position which carried a certain amount of authority: they considered me a little young.

I, in turn, found it strange to have a young girl working under me as between-maid. Her name was Mary and she was a quick and willing worker and made it easy for us to fit in well together. She was pretty with fair, curly hair, a ready smile and was always eager to please. She lived with her parents and family in the village, only a short distance away so it was convenient for her to slip home in her free time.

I had a pretty bedroom to myself as well as other privileges: I had more free time and was able to renew my friendship with Miss Gracie the Girl Guide Lieutenant. I soon bought a bicycle for a modest sum; it was a real boon as it was really the only way to get to and from the towns. There were no local buses and we could not afford taxi fares. My cycle and I did many miles around the district. In those days there was no fear of travelling alone. Apart from Miss Gracie I had no other friends in the district. St. Faiths had left Parkstone and a smaller Home had been started in Surrey.

As time went on I grew to enjoy the work; I was no longer nervous to try out dishes or plan menus even when visitors came to stay.

After a year a very embarrassing thing happened to me; for some unknown reason lumps and bumps appeared on my hands and face and other parts of my body. These irritated and burned and would come up in minutes even around my eyes and between my fingers. I went to see a doctor; once again the ladies frowned on me because of this peculiar state of affairs. I could not make pastry or anything that needed direct handling. It was even suggested that I wear cotton gloves. The doctor could not identify these mystery spots although he said they were not contagious and called them 'rheumatic manifestations'.

Time passed and my progress was steady rather than spectacular. I began to feel the need for change. As fortune would have it, a young man entered my life about this time. One day I was window shopping in Poole during one of my free afternoons. Suddenly I heard my name called and hurrying towards me was a smiling woman pushing a pretty fair-haired child. It was Daisy, who had been one of the older girls from St. Faiths. We had not formed any special friendship at that time so we had lost touch with each other. Of course, we had much news to exchange and Daisy insisted that I go back with her and her daughter Ivy to have tea and meet her husband.

They lived in a council house in Upper Parkstone. It was a change to have somewhere definite to go and I slipped into the homely atmosphere easily. We had a pleasant tea. Daisy's husband was a sharp-eyed and lively young man, fond of a joke, but with an uncertain temper which she seemed able to cope with and understand. I left with a light heart to cycle back to Lilliput and this was the first of many visits. Later Ivy had a brother, Edwin, named after Daisy's brother who was killed in the War.

Some months later, Daisy said that her husband's brother was due to have some leave and that she would like me to meet him. He was in the R.A.S.C. stationed at Aldershot. I was not sure that I particularly wanted to meet him. His name was Charles and he was due home in a fortnight. I've since realised that Daisy had it all carefully planned.

One day she invited me round and I was well involved in a game with Ivy. I was lying on the settee with Ivy riding on my drawn-up knees; my hair was pulled across my face for the horse's mane. Suddenly the door opened and in walked a very smart good-looking chap in khaki. Then Daisy appeared and introduced us. I left rather earlier than usual, but Charles asked if he could see me again before his leave was up. I did not give him a definite answer but secretly hoped we should meet again. We did not fall in love at first sight, but our friendship gave me something to look forward to instead of always wandering about on my own.

We courted for several months and met whenever he had leave; letters took the place of meetings when he was back in Barracks. We were glad of each other's company as neither of us had many friends. Eventually I decided to leave my post at

Lilliput and move nearer to Aldershot: in those days it was easy to find another job. I worked as a 'temporary' to an officer and his wife in Farnham. Charles and I spent our free time together. One wet day when neither of us had anywhere to go I invited Charles into the warmth of the kitchen for a cup of tea. The officer's wife saw him there and was very angry. I would have been dismissed on the spot if I had not been the only cook she had had who could manage to make toast on the three-burner oil stove and who knew how to clean and fit it properly! She warned me that there would be dire consequences if I entertained a 'follower' in her kitchen again. I consoled myself that it was only a short-term engagement.

There followed a succession of temporary jobs around the district. I walked out of one situation because the food was so poor: the lady of the house expected to feed the staff on the rations allowed to her and her husband, yet spent money like water on lavish dinner parties to impress her friends. The taxi driver who took me to the station when I left the job said that I was the third one to leave that particular house in the last couple of months.

I moved on to a grand looking house in a village in Surrey. I was intrigued by a dinner service that was seldom used. The dinner plates had an inscription in a soft shade of blue: 'Better a dinner of herbs where love is, than a roasted ox and hatred withal'.

Eventually I left the district around Farnham and returned to become a cook in a house in Mount Road, Parkstone: it was the house which had once been used as a hospital for officers during the War. It was a pleasant situation; there were two other maids and a 'daily' to do the rough work. The house had a happy atmosphere about it. I have often been aware of this peculiarity concerning houses: some have a definite aura about them even as one approaches them. I have wondered since whether this particular house was specially blessed. The lady and her family were very musical; she had a sound-proof room built, and members of the staff were invited to go in and listen when she and her friends were rehearsing; they played during the afternoon tea-sessions at the Winter Gardens in Bournemouth, a ladylike performance enhancing the gracious and tranquil atmosphere of Afternoon Teatime.

Not long after this a cloud rose on the horizon: it seemed possible that Charles might be drafted abroad. So we decided to get married. We were unable to find a room to rent that we could afford and so it was arranged that Charles would have to return to his digs in Poole and I would return to my work as cook for a short while.

In 1927, on a bright summer's day, Charles and I were married. My dress was made of a pretty blue, soft linen with a pleated skirt, and was decorated with three triangles of blue braid. I wore a cloche hat in a pinky-beige colour. Charles wore his uniform. Only Daisy and a maid with whom I worked were our witnesses. Edna Wright became the wife of Private Charles Henry Mould, a Tradesman of the R.A.S.C., at a church in Poole in the county of Dorset - dear little Dorset. After the brief ceremony we had a small celebration at Daisy's house. That evening Charles and I went out and sat together on Constitution Hill eating cherries.

Edna and Violet posing on the cradle-shaped chair